Through A Dark Silence:

Loving and Living with Your Blind and Deaf Dog

Debbie Bauer

Dedicated to Lady …

She was beautiful – just ten months old. Her long white Collie coat was just starting to resemble what it was to become. She lived in an outdoor pen with a couple trees and a shed to offer protection for her and the other adolescent Collies she lived with. She always greeted me like I was her friend.

I had been told she was different. I was to feed her away from the others and watch to be sure they didn't eat her food. I always put her bowl down first and used the other bowls to lead the rest of the pups to another area of the pen, leaving her a few extra moments to eat her meal. Although, she never seemed to lose any time eating, that's for sure!

Lady knew no manners when I met her. As far as I could tell, she had never left her pen. She became my summer project that year. I hurried to get my kennel chores done so I could spend time with her on my breaks.

I taught her to walk on a leash, to go up and down stairs, and even to hop over a low bar hurdle. She learned to fetch a toy, to sit and lie down, shake hands, and to come when called. She learned not to jump on me and how to stand quietly for grooming. She learned to be my friend.

I grew to love her over that summer. When my kennel job was over for the summer, I offered to buy Lady and give her a good home. I expected they would be happy to have found Lady a home. You see, Lady had been both blind and deaf from birth – the product of a merle to merle breeding.

In my youth and ignorance, I had assumed that this was just a fluke – an isolated case. But the breeders would not sell her to me. They wanted to keep her for their breeding program. My heart broke that day as I had to say goodbye to my new friend. I knew that she would start the next day waiting for me to come to her. I never saw Lady again.

I had no idea back then that one day I would be rescuing other dogs like Lady. I have always kept her close in my heart as one of my own dogs. Today I am able to educate others about the dangers of breeding merle to merle litters.

And so, I dedicate this book to Lady's memory. She showed me that she was a dog first – a dog like all the others. No one told me she couldn't be taught things just like the other dogs. And so, we taught each other. Thank you, Lady … this book is for you!

Contents

Welcome!

Whether you are contemplating the decision to adopt a blind and deaf (b/d) dog, or you already live with one, this book can offer valuable information and assistance. There are many reasons why a dog may be blind and deaf – old age, progressive disease, injury, genetics, etc. Some dogs are b/d since birth, while others come upon it as they age.

Dogs that are losing their sight and hearing due to age or progressive conditions have already learned to rely on those senses to gather information about their surroundings. It may be scary for them to begin to lose that information. They may need more careful handling and care as they learn to rely more on their other senses and trust that new input.

If possible, introduce the tools and suggestions in this book while your dog still has some vision and hearing left, so she will learn to rely on new ways of obtaining information. She will learn to identify her surroundings through vibrations, air currents, smells and touch. As she comes to rely on these tools more and more, her transition will become easier.

Dogs that are blind and deaf from birth learn from the time they are puppies to rely on their other senses. They start exploring right away along with their littermates. They learn to map out new areas with their senses of smell and touch. I will talk a lot in this book about dogs that have been blind and deaf since birth.

Most of my experience working with and living with b/d dogs involves those dogs being homozygous merles. This means they carry two copies of the merle pattern gene. These dogs are often called double merles, and that is how I will refer to them throughout this book. The visual and hearing impairments that occur with double merles are completely preventable through education and proper breeding practices.

There are many variations of blindness and deafness in dogs, even within the scope of double merles. A dog may be totally blind and deaf, but my experience is that most dogs have varying degrees of vision and/or hearing loss. That makes each one an individual case. You will need to adjust your training and day to day handling of your dog to utilize whatever qualities of sight and/or hearing she does have. You will find varying suggestions throughout this book to assist you with deciding which methods are best for you and your dog.

This is not an exact science. Each dog is an individual and cannot be grouped into one category, just because she is considered blind and deaf. This book is not meant to be the only way to communicate with a b/d dog. It is meant to serve as a guidebook to give you tips and guidance along the way. If something does not work for you and your dog, feel free to adapt it or try something else. It is only by trying that we find out if it will work or not!

Things to Consider Before Adopting a B/D Dog

Bringing a new dog into your home is always an adjustment. Bringing in a dog with special needs is an even bigger adjustment. Adopting a blind and deaf dog is not the right option for everyone; anymore than dog ownership is right for everyone. For many, though, it can be a very positive experience. In this section of the book, I will try to give you an overview of information to help you with the decision as to whether this is the right choice for you right now.

You must first consider if you can commit the time and money necessary to give a dog what she needs for the next 10-20 years. Dogs are living longer in many cases, and it's not fair to take on a new dog without having the resources to care for it for its entire life.

Every dog should be adopted forever. Can you imagine losing everyone and everything you had ever loved? You are your dog's world. It's devastating for her to lose that security. A b/d dog relies on you for her safety and security. In her world, you are her constant. Please do not make the decision to adopt unless you are totally committed to a lifelong relationship with this dog.

You should consider the breed or mix of breeds involved. A b/d dog is a dog first and then an individual second, way before the special needs even come into play. Some breeds are bred to be always busy. Are you prepared to keep your dog constantly exercised and stimulated? She may become a trouble-maker if her energy and brain are not channeled in the right direction.

If you need help deciding if a certain breed or mix is the right choice for you, there are many resources out there about different dog breeds and how to choose the right dog for you. Take some time to research them. Please remember that b/d dogs need everything that other dogs need first and foremost. And then, most need a little bit more.

More about double merles

One all too common cause of blindness and deafness in dogs is breeding two merle-patterned dogs together. There are many terms used to describe these dogs – homozygous merle, lethal white, and double merle are just a few. What makes the double merles worth special mention is that this category of disability can be totally prevented. The only way a double merle is created is by breeding together two dogs that each carry the merle gene. By not breeding two merle dogs together, the risk of creating double merle puppies can be completely avoided. (In the picture below, the dog on the left is a blue merle, while the dog on the right is a double merle.)

There are many breeds of dogs that can carry the merle gene. Sometimes the merle gene has a different name in different breeds, but the gene still reacts the same when it is doubled up. Some of these breeds are: Cocker Spaniels, Australian Shepherds, Shetland Sheepdogs, Border Collies, Chihuahuas, Collies, and Dachshunds. There are others, and some breeders are trying to introduce the merle gene into different breeds all the time.

The merle pattern gene causes a dilution of color, resulting in a coat showing many shades of color patterns. There is nothing wrong with the merle gene if it is handled responsibly. Breeding a merle to a non-merle dog can give us the popular mottled look and can give us healthy and sound dogs, while breeding merle to merle often produces puppies with severe impairments.

Many double merles may be deaf or hearing-impaired to some degree. Hair cells in the inner ear need to have pigment in order for the dog to hear. Without pigment, the nerve endings do not develop properly and the dog will be deaf or partially deaf. Looking at the color on the dog's outer ear is not an indicator. The inner ear cannot be seen by the human eye. It is way down inside the ear canal. A dog can have a white outer ear but still be able to hear if the inner ear has pigment. It can also have a colored ear and be deaf.

Many double merles have eye defects as well. These defects can occur in any color of eye, but may be easier to see in lighter colored eyes. The actual size and shape of the eye may be affected. Some have smaller than usual eyes. Some have pupils that are irregularly shaped. Pupils may have jagged or spiky edges, look like starbursts, and/or be different sizes and appear to have pieces missing from the darker pigmented areas of the eye. Eyes may be very sensitive to light if the pupil does not react properly.

Some pupils appear to be in the wrong place in the eye and it may look like the dog is looking in a different direction than where she is facing. Some dogs may appear to have no eyes, or may have eyes covered by the third eyelid permanently. Dogs with affected eyes may show a combination of these defects. Any of these eye defects can cause varying degrees of visual impairment, including blindness. (On the next page are some pictures showing differences in eyes of some double merles.)

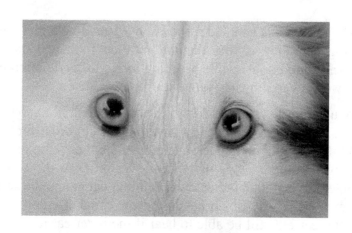

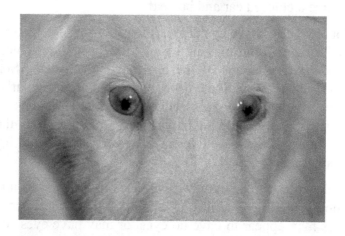

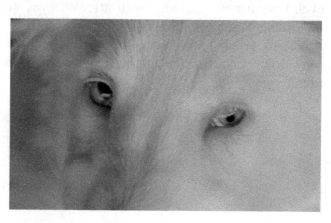

Double merles require all the same things as other dogs. They need good quality food, veterinary care, walks and exercise, playtime and mental stimulation, grooming, management, supervision, and training. They will need to be housetrained and taught what not to chew. Yes, they shed just like other dogs do, and yes, deaf dogs do bark! They dig and they destroy things sometimes too, just like any other dog.

Often double merles need even more than the average dog. They may need more veterinary care depending upon the impairments caused by poor breeding practices. They need more supervision at times. You will need to be much more aware of keeping your dog safe, because she cannot see or hear trouble coming and will be at a disadvantage. Playtime and exercise may need to be done differently depending upon the dog's abilities. You will most likely need to learn a new way of training and communicating with your b/d dog. Sometimes b/d dogs require new or different equipment and adaptations made to her environment to ensure her safety and quality of life. This goes for any b/d dog, not just double merles.

Many double merles are finding themselves homeless and unwanted. Please help to educate others about the dangers of merle to merle breedings. If you are a member of a breed club for a breed where merle (or a related gene) is a known pattern, please make educational materials available to your members, breeders and the public as they consider a dog of your breed. If you are a trainer, shelter worker, or rescue group, please educate yourself in techniques to train deaf, blind, and b/d dogs, so you will be available to help owners.

Some myths about b/d dogs discussed

There are some myths surrounding b/d dogs. Unfortunately, these misconceptions often prevent some marvelous dogs from being adopted. Here are some that I hear most often:

Adopting a blind or deaf dog will be a huge burden.

While living with a blind, deaf, or b/d dog is different in the beginning, once you learn how to set up the environment to make it easier for you and your dog, there is not much extra that needs to be done. You must always supervise your b/d dog for safety reasons, but this is not so different from supervising any other dog. Having lived with many b/d and deaf dogs, I would say it is not a burden. It is not any harder than living with other dogs, it is just different.

Deaf (or blind) dogs will bite if startled or woken up.

Some people assume that a deaf dog will startle easily and will be prone to biting. Deaf dogs adapt very well to their hearing loss. They learn routines and expectations in the home where they live. Yes, a deaf dog can startle by an unexpected touch. Hearing dogs startle from unexpected touches, too. It is just harder to sneak up on and startle a hearing dog because it can hear you coming. Most dogs, deaf or hearing, that startle, do not turn and bite. They will jump a bit and then turn to see what is going on.

It is important to remember that snapping and biting are a normal way of communicating for dogs. Most dogs will not snap or bite without providing other warning communications first. If their other, more subtle, ways of communicating are ignored, they will then progress to snapping, and finally, to biting, if they feel the need to protect themselves. It is up to us, as the humans in their lives, to teach our dogs (hearing or deaf) the behaviors that we consider acceptable.

There are ways to help dogs become more comfortable with being touched and woken up. Some of these will be discussed later in this book. But it's also important to be courteous when waking your deaf dog. Think about yourself when someone wakes you from a sound sleep. It is much nicer to be awakened gradually than suddenly startled awake. The same is true for your dog.

Tap your feet a bit from a distance as you approach to give off a vibration through the floor. Sneaking up on a sleeping dog and then stomping is also very startling, so start at a distance and just walk a bit heavier than normal as you approach. The vibration will be stronger as you get closer and usually will wake your dog. Blowing gently on your dog can also help her wake up gradually. Always reward your dog after waking her up to help her associate being woken up with good things.

Double merle dogs have many medical issues.

Many people think that double merles cannot be healthy and will have a whole host of medical issues. While it is true that some double merles do have other health and medical conditions, I am aware of no research stating that these issues are a result of breeding merle to merle. Dogs that are not double merles can also have a multitude of health issues.

However, many people who breed merle to merle litters are not concerned with proper breeding practices and doing genetic and other health clearances on their dogs. Getting a dog from an unknown genetic past is always an unknown. That being said, there are many double merles with no other health issues than visual and hearing impairments. They are perfectly healthy in every other way and live long happy lives.

Cognitive ability is affected in b/d dogs.

Some people think a deaf dog may be difficult to train. Giving voice commands to our dogs is a human preference. Dogs don't care much about spoken words. They are much more tuned into watching our body language and visual cues. That is the language they share with each other, so it comes naturally to them. Our visual cues stand out to dogs much more than our words do.

Deaf dogs are very observant. They will take their cues from the environment and those in it, and will respond just as quickly. They will respond to vibrations they feel around them. They will learn what even your smallest body movements mean – just by observing! It is very easy to teach them hand signals and other visual cues.

Dogs that are b/d will be more challenging to communicate with, but they will learn quickly if you are consistent. They won't respond to the same visual cues in their environment as other dogs. For this reason, they are often labeled as unintelligent, stubborn, or bad, and then they are often secluded and ignored. Their cognitive ability is the same as that of other dogs, but often, no one tries to communicate with a b/d dog, thinking the dog is not capable of doing certain things. It is also important to give b/d dogs the same socialization to new experiences as other dogs are given, especially during puppyhood when the brain is still developing. If the brain's cells are not used and challenged, they will not grow and develop.

If you adopt a blind and deaf dog, you need to be able to stay home with the dog all the time.

I have seen this so many times on the profile of a dog that is b/d and is in need of adoption. I wonder how many amazing homes were turned down because that person had to go to work or had other commitments outside the home.

Blind/deaf dogs can be taught to stay home comfortably by themselves, just like any other dog. It is true that some of them have separation anxiety, but many dogs that can see and hear just fine also have separation issues. In fact, it is one of the most common behavior issues reported in dog family households. Dogs must be taught and conditioned to stay alone calmly. This is a gradual process.

Dogs are social animals and enjoy having company, so no dog should be expected to be alone for long periods of time on a regular basis. But for normal household schedules, there is no reason to expect that someone should be home with a b/d dog all the time. There are many enrichment activities discussed in this book that can be used to keep the dog busy while you're gone.

You must have another dog that can see and hear if you adopt a b/d dog.

Here is another myth I have seen on some profiles of b/d dogs needing homes. Dogs enjoy company, but a b/d dog can be quite content without another dog in the home. Blind/deaf dogs can get along with other dogs (hearing, seeing, deaf, blind, or blind/deaf) just the same as hearing and seeing dogs. Each dog, b/d or otherwise, is an individual and may get along with some dogs and not others. The preferences of your dog should always be considered when adding a new dog to the family.

Some dogs do form special bonds in which a dog that can see and hear may take on the role of a guide for the b/d dog. While this makes for a great story, it is not the norm. More often, the dogs will form bonds and friendships amongst themselves and they will just treat each other like they treat any other dog. While it can be nice to have more than one dog, there is no reason to feel like you must have another dog in order to adopt a b/d dog.

Sometimes in a rescue situation, a b/d dog may be offered for adoption along with another dog that she has already learned to rely on. In these situations, I do agree that it is kinder for the dogs to be adopted together, as they already have a bond together.

Safety considerations with a b/d dog

A dog that is blind and deaf needs to have some special safety considerations taken into account. Her safety needs to always be a priority. This is something that will need to continue for the dog's entire lifetime. At first, these may seem overwhelming as you're trying to remember them all at once, but soon they will become just second nature to you and will become part of your normal routine. You won't even need to think about them, because they have just become a part of how you interact with your b/d dog.

Off leash freedom

A b/d dog should never be let off leash unless she is in a fully enclosed area. She is still a dog and can be easily distracted in any direction at any time. I am constantly amazed at how quickly my b/d dogs get around outdoors when they are following a scent. Always check doors and gates to make sure they are secure.

I know there are some people who do allow their b/d dogs off leash in unfenced areas, but it is always a risk. It is safer to keep your dog in an enclosed area or use a leash. Yes, your b/d dog may tend to stick very close and you may think she would never run off. Just remember that she is a dog first and anything could distract her. If your b/d wandered off, the chances of getting her back safely are slim. There are long lightweight leashes that can be used to give your dog lots of freedom in unfenced areas, but will still allow you to regain control of the situation quickly if anything unforeseen happens.

Supervision with other dogs

Another important safety consideration is that b/d dogs cannot recognize normal dog-to-dog communication signals. They are not able to hear a growl or other vocalizations, nor are they able to see the other dog's body language that says, "Stay away!" Because of this, b/d dogs can get into trouble with other dogs. In a dog's world, there is a code to follow. Just like in human society, there are responses that are considered polite, and not so polite.

Other dogs may not understand why your b/d dog is bumping into them or intruding on their space. Personal space is very important in dog-dog communication. Some dogs require more space than others. Other dogs may see this behavior as rude. Dogs normally reprimand other dogs whose behavior is rude. They do this with their mouths. If a dog reprimands another dog, it is not being mean or doing anything wrong. That is its normal way of communicating. You must keep your b/d dog safe.

Many b/d dogs get along very well with other dogs. But you need to be aware that your b/d dog is at a disadvantage in reading and responding to normal dog body language and behavior. She will also not be able to see to get out of the way if other dogs around her get into a scuffle. If your b/d dog is playing with other dogs, she won't be able to hear if the other dog yelps because she bit too hard in play. Always be nearby and ready to intervene if necessary.

It is safest to separate your b/d dog from other dogs when you need to go away and leave them alone. This includes dogs that your b/d dog lives with on a daily basis. Many dogs may learn to be tolerant of the b/d dog as they realize she's not a threat. However, dogs communicate with each other constantly. They expect other dogs to respond appropriately to these communications. A dog that does not respond appropriately will be disciplined. Even without meaning any harm, a dog can injure your b/d dog, because she won't be able to see the discipline coming and get out of the way. Putting up a gate will allow the dogs to be near each other, even lying next to each other on either side of the gate, while you are gone, but will ensure your b/d dog stays safe.

Taking your b/d dog to a dog park could be a very bad idea. No doubt, there are b/d dogs who do fine in that environment. But there are often dogs at dog parks that will not have been exposed to b/d dogs and won't have experience with their mannerisms. Also, active dogs often run into each other in play and a b/d would not be able to brace herself or get out of the way and could be seriously injured by a larger dog bowling her over. If you must use a dog park to exercise your b/d dog, try to find times when the park is not crowded and when smaller and quieter dogs are there.

Dog-proofing and other considerations for your home

Your home will need to be dog-proofed. Dangerous areas such as pools, steps, and balconies should always be blocked off unless you are closely and directly supervising. Blind/deaf dogs can learn to swim and do steps safely, but they should never be left alone with these possible dangers when no one is there with them. Many decks and in-home landings have railings with spaces where a smaller dog may be able to fall through. Attaching a mesh barrier securely around the railings will keep your dog safe and prevent falls.

On walks, a b/d dog cannot see things on her eye level which may poke her like branches from bushes. You will need to direct her around sign posts, hydrants, curbs, etc. She will not see other people and dogs approaching. You will need to watch out for and manage these situations carefully.

The safest way to transport your b/d dog by car is with a crate or a dog seatbelt. She won't be able to see the drop off when you open the car door and she may be in a hurry and jump or fall out. She also won't be able to see loose items coming towards her or where she is in space if you stop short or get into an accident. Ensure that a crate is secure or that the seatbelt will prevent her from falling off the seat.

Try not to startle your b/d dog unnecessarily. Sometimes a startle just can't be helped, but try to always be aware of when something may startle her, and find a different way to do it. Think about how you feel when you are startled. It's not a pleasant feeling and it puts you on edge for a while afterwards. The same is true for your dog. And if she gets startled often enough, it may trigger defensive behavior in your dog, such as snapping or biting. Make sure guests know not to sneak up on your dog. Be ready to intervene if necessary.

Sun exposure

Many double merles are mostly white with pink skin and noses that are prone to sunburn. This is especially true of short-haired dogs and dogs with white faces where the hair is shorter and thinner. It is important to minimize exposure to heavy sunlight and to use a sunscreen that is non-toxic and safe for pets.

Put the sunscreen on your hands first and then rub it into the dog's face, ears, and nose. If you are going to be outside for an extended period of time, remember to reapply the sunscreen periodically. Stay in the shade as much as possible during the brightest parts of the day. A short-haired dog can also wear a lightweight T-shirt to help protect her body from the sun. Some dogs will learn to wear a hat with a brim to keep the sun away from their eyes. There is also dog eye gear that can protect sensitive eyes from the sun.

Expectations

Wow, there is so much to consider! Don't let yourself get overwhelmed. Some things can be put in place, like the dog-proofing suggestions, and then you're finished with it. Other things, you will learn as you go along. Try to pick just one or two things to focus on at a time.

I want to talk a bit about expectations. We are only limited by the expectations we put on ourselves and our dogs. The possibilities along this journey you are on are endless! If you truly believe that, you will be surprised every day by what your b/d dog can achieve!

If your dog was born blind and deaf, this is her normal. She has no idea that she is "challenged" and "different" from other dogs. It is our perspective as humans that gets in the way and causes us to feel badly for her. Your dog will remain intent on being the normal dog she believes she is. Your job is to allow her to be that normal dog as much as possible.

If your dog is losing her sight and hearing later in life, be understanding and try to help her adjust to these new changes in her life. Dogs are very adaptable to change if we give them a chance to be. Your dog may not understand the changes going on in her life, but I'm pretty sure she doesn't want to just sit around and do nothing. She wants to continue getting the most out of every day. She may need some help from you in the beginning, but allow her to adjust and find new ways of doing things. Feeling sorry for her won't help her to make progress, but believing in her and helping her will.

There will be people (many people) you meet that just don't understand. They will feel sorry for your "poor dog." They will wonder what kind of enjoyment your dog could possibly have in her life. Try to educate these people, but don't stand around and dwell on their opinions. Allow your b/d dog to live her life to the fullest, and you will begin to change their minds and their hearts when they see what she is capable of. Your dog will become an inspiration to them.

Don't allow the expectations of others to limit you or your dog! Don't give up if you run into a road block. Find a solution that works for you and your dog. Help your b/d dog become the best she can be. The possibilities are endless!

Questions About Treasure

Treasure is the b/d dog that accompanies me out and about the most. There are many questions that I'm asked over and over again about her. These are the public's most pressing concerns when they find out Treasure is blind and deaf. Perhaps you have some of these same questions on your mind as you are considering adopting a b/d dog. Or perhaps you've heard these same questions asked about your own b/d dog. Or, maybe still, like many people, you just want to know more about Treasure!

How old is she?

Almost always, when people find out Treasure is blind and deaf, they want to know how old she is. They assume that she must be blind and deaf because she's an older dog that has lost her sensory abilities. They are surprised to know that she is fairly young. At the time of this writing, she is seven years old. Treasure is a double merle sheltie and has been blind and deaf since birth.

How does she get around?

Treasure walks and trots around the house and yard just like my other dogs. She knows the layout. She has a mental map similar to a GPS inside her head. She can feel the difference between carpet and tile and throw rugs. These things that I hardly notice in my day to day activities are very important to her. She can sense immediately where the wooden ramp in the backyard begins and ends, and she knows every dip in the ground outside. Each of these things let her know where she is in space, so she knows which way to turn to get to where she wants to go. Most of the time, she barely even pauses and if you were watching her, you would swear that she can see where she's going. And, of course, she also knows her way around by smells.

Does she run into things?

Yes, she does on occasion, but for the most part, she can smell and sense when she's near someone or something. I keep the furniture layout pretty much the same, as well as where I keep the dog bowls and her crate. She can find them easily. But she adapts very quickly to new obstacles in her way – the Christmas tree, a chair pulled out away from the table, or a box placed here or there.

Treasure is exceptional at feeling air currents and pressure. She will usually slow herself as she gets closer to walls and will begin sniffing and searching for the barrier, so her bump is usually a softer one - or none at all. I think she notices that the air currents and scents are different near a large obstacle or barrier and, so, is able to maneuver around them. Smaller obstacles, like things on the floor, she will bump into more often.

Is she housetrained? How does she tell you that she needs to go outside?

Many people are curious about Treasure's housetraining habits. Doing one's business is not dependent upon sight or hearing. There are times when I find my way to the bathroom in the middle of the night without turning on a light.

I housetrained her just like my other dogs – with a schedule and positive reinforcement for going where I wanted her to go. If I caught her starting to go inside, I would interrupt her and take her outside to finish. Because Treasure is b/d, I use touch and soft petting to praise her, which meant that I had to stay close to her while she did her business so I could let her know with petting when she was right.

Treasure is very aware of when she is inside or outside. The smells are very different, as are the surfaces. She can easily tell the difference between grass and carpet, or grass and tile. Pay attention the next time you open a door leading to the outside. Feel the rush of fresh air hit your face, smell the outside smells, feel the temperature change on your skin and the sunshine on your body. There are so many cues that you are going from inside to outside.

Treasure does her business on a schedule usually, but she will also ask me to go out if she needs to by jumping up on my leg, or by going to the back door. I also taught Treasure to do her business on touch cue, so when we are out doing a therapy visit, I can give her the opportunity to go before we go inside. It also comes in handy when traveling, or when the weather is cold or rainy!

How do your other dogs get along with her?

People always want to know how my other dogs get along with Treasure. Strangely, they don't often ask how she gets along with them. What they really want to know when questioned is do my other dogs know that she's blind and deaf, and do they treat her any differently?

I do think my dogs know that Treasure communicates and gathers information differently. Thankfully, they are very patient and tolerant of her, but I can't say that they truly treat her differently.

Each of my dogs has a unique relationship with each of the other dogs. They behave differently with the elderly dog than they do with the puppy, and they have their own special buddies. So, in that way, they treat Treasure like they treat the others.

They don't offer her any special advantages. They will still take her bone or goodies if they think they can get away with it. The puppy will jump on her when she's relaxing, just like he does to the others.

When the gang's excited, they will push her aside, but they do the same to each other.

They have learned to alter their behavior toward Treasure in some circumstances. The puppy has learned that the best way to get Treasure to play with him is for him to maintain a lot of body-to-body contact with her. In this way, she will know where he is and will continue to play with him. If he just taps her and bounces away, she doesn't know where he went and soon tires of the game. The dogs have learned that if she bumps into them, she doesn't mean any harm, yet if they bump into each other, there are sometimes words exchanged.

Does she know the other dogs can see and hear?

I really don't know for sure, but Treasure was born both blind and deaf and doesn't know any differently. To her, she is normal just like they are. But, again, she will treat them just like any other dog. She will help herself to their bones and goodies if she thinks she can get away with it. She will push her way into the group to get to me first when I am handing out goodies or she wants to be petted.

What's wrong with her eyes? Can she see anything at all?

Treasure has a condition called microphthalmia. Her actual eyes are smaller than normal and so are recessed farther into the eye sockets. This allows the third eyelid to spread across and cover her eyes, causing them to look pink. She does have eyes underneath the third eyelid and thus is able to see the difference in light and darkness. She cannot see movement or objects unless they cast a shadow that she will then see as the difference between light and dark. She has no functional vision, and can only see very drastic changes in light and dark.

How does she eat her food?

Treasure eats from a shallow bowl and will use her tongue to scoop up the food along the outside edge of the bowl to her mouth. By keeping her mouth in contact with the outer edge of the bowl, she always knows where the bowl is in space and it prevents her from bumping her mouth on it as she takes each bite. She does the same thing when she drinks water.

Treasure eats her meals in a crate, so that she is safe to eat at her own speed without the other dogs trying to sneak any from her. This also helps her not to get protective of her food because she does not feel as if she has to defend her meal or gulp it down quickly in order to protect it.

Does she bark?

Yes, Treasure does bark. She will sometimes bark when she is insecure and doesn't know where I am. She doesn't do this much anymore but did it a lot in the beginning of our relationship. She will bark when she gets excited, such as when I come home or when it's mealtime and she doesn't want to wait. Every once in a while she will bark when she is playing. But usually her play noise is more like a soft mumbling noise. Overall, she is a very quiet dog.

Does she know who you are?

Treasure knows my scent and knows the difference between my scent and someone else's. She remembers people she has met before. She gets excited when I arrive home or enter a room she has been snoozing in. She will follow me around from room to room. She likes to be included in whatever I'm doing whether I'm folding laundry, or cleaning, or reading or typing. She is a socialite and enjoys meeting new people, but she will stop to find out where I am before continuing. If she is insecure with someone, she will avoid them and stick to me like glue. But this does not happen very often. She is a very self-confident girl.

Do you have to keep everything in its place?

Yes and no. I keep the big stuff like furniture in basically the same place, and I keep her bowls and crate and steps in the same place all the time. Things get moved around the yard and I am not a neat freak, so there is always a bit of clutter around the house and on the floors, not to mention dog toys and bones scattered all over the floor. Treasure gets around fine and doesn't have any trouble. If something new appears, she is the first one to check it out and she will rarely bump into it more than once or twice. She enjoys having new things to explore and even something that is not new but moved to a new spot, like my shoes, will deserve her investigation.

22

I also take Treasure with me when I travel, so she often has to map out new hotel rooms and other new environments. She does this quickly and eagerly, always wanting to check out the new smells and such.

Does she play with toys?

She does play with toys. Sometimes she will bite at and shake a stuffed toy that she finds, and she chews on bones. But she doesn't chase toys and play fetch. She can't see the toys moving to chase them and she can't hear them squeak or fall on the floor. Treasure didn't have toys as a younger dog, so she really didn't learn how to play with them. But she does like to chew on bones. Sometimes she will find other things to chew on – her favorites are wicker baskets! I utilize food toys and puzzles to play with Treasure. She likes to eat and can smell the food, so when I put the food inside the toys and puzzles, she will interact with the toys to get the food out. She enjoys puzzles that make her think and problem solve.

Is she an albino?

There are many terms used to describe double merle dogs. The one I hear misused the most is albino. I think many people think that any white dog must be an albino, but this is not correct. An albino is actually a rather rare phenomenon. An albino has pale pink skin and eyes with absolutely no pigment. The eyes will appear to be pink. Albinos have no color or spots at all. If the dog is white but has dark or colored eyes, it is not an albino. If there is any color on the dog at all, it is not an albino. Double merles often have spots or areas of color on their bodies and usually have some pigment in their eyes. They are not albino.

Sometimes people use the term lethal white. The term lethal white originated in the horse world. There is a lethal gene in some paint horses that results in an all-white foal. The gene causes a condition which does not allow the foal to digest food. The foal dies within hours or days of birth. Thus, the term lethal. Double merles are able to digest food and live a normal life span. They do not carry the lethal white gene.

The correct technical term is homozygous merle, which simply means there are two copies of the merle gene. The term double merle is easier to remember but does state the same thing – there is a double dose of the merle gene. I use the term double merle because it is easy for most people to remember and to visualize.

Do you have to carry her everywhere? Does she ever get out of her stroller?

When most people see Treasure, she is riding in her stroller. She rides in her stroller for pet therapy visits and in new crowded environments. It keeps her safely up off the floor where people might trip on her. She's small and can't see people coming towards her to move out of the way. Being up higher in the stroller also helps people to see her better. I can roll the stroller up beside someone's chair and the person can easily reach out to pet her on their level without needing to stoop or bend over.

I am fortunate that Treasure is small enough for me to pick up easily. It comes in handy for getting her through certain areas safely, like across streets or parking lots, where there is a lot to watch out for. But I don't carry her everywhere. Treasure loves to explore and sniff around, just like most other dogs. She can walk on a leash with me, and where it is safely fenced, I can let her explore off leash with me nearby.

How do you communicate with her?

I use touch to communicate with Treasure. Everything you would normally say or gesture to other dogs, I tell her with my touch. I tell her when I'm going to take her outside, or for a ride in the car. I tell her when it's mealtime. I tell her I love her. I tell her she's done something that I like. I tell her when it's time for her nails to be cut, and when it's time for bed.

How did you train her? How does she know what you want?

Dogs don't start out knowing what we want them to do. They need to be taught and then rewarded when they do things that we like. They don't start out understanding English, so teaching a b/d dog is no different from teaching any other dog. They both need to be shown and taught what we expect. We can teach them verbal cues, signal cues, or touch cues, but the process is still the same.

I showed Treasure what I wanted her to do and practiced it with her. I rewarded her when she got it right and I repeated things when they didn't go as planned until we got them right. I added touch cues just like most people would add a verbal cue. By putting the cue together with the behavior over and over again, she learned that they went together.

Will I scare her if I pet her?

No, Treasure loves petting! But you might startle her if you touch her and she didn't realize your hand was coming towards her. Letting her smell your hand briefly before touching her will prevent her from being startled. Please start to pet her gently on the shoulder or side of her neck. She doesn't appreciate a big hand suddenly plunking down on the top of her head and she will duck away for a moment in surprise. Once you have started petting her, you can move your hand up to her head if you wish. She will be able to follow the feel of your hand on her body to know where you are reaching for next.

Why do her ears move and prick forward? Are you sure she can't hear anything?

Ear positions in dogs don't always mean they are hearing noises. Dogs will prick their ears forward if they are alert and interested in something. Treasure does the same. If she is annoyed with the puppy, she will draw her ears back against the sides of her head. If she is relaxed, they will droop to the sides a bit. If she feels vibrations or changes in air current or scent, her ears will prick up and forward as she investigates. Often those ear movements correlate to noises that we hear. But noises often include vibrations and movement (which move air currents and scent around). It's easy to second guess and think that Treasure actually "heard" something when she didn't. But she did notice it!

Why does she spin in circles like that?

There are several situations in which Treasure will spin in small circles. Her spin changes slightly in each situation and I have learned what they mean. She will spin very fast when she is excited about me coming home or when I release her to play the game of nosework that she loves. When she is investigating a new or interesting smell, she will spin slower with her nose pointing up and her mouth barely open to take in as much scent as possible. She will spin and then stop and then spin and then stop. When I first put her down in an area, she will spin a few times to get her bearings and then will head off in the direction she wants to go. As I watch her, I think she uses circling in that context to feel out her environment. It is nicer to bump into something with your side and gently brush past it than to run into something head on. So, until she realizes where she is and can tell that there is nothing solid in her path, she circles, then when the coast is clear, she goes straight ahead.

Is it hard to live with her? She must be a burden to you.

Treasure is such a blessing to me. There are things that I do differently with Treasure than with my other dogs, but she is not burdensome. Things are just different. At first it took a lot of my energy to think about and remember these things, just because they were different than what I was used to. But this is all just part of the routine now. I hardly think about the things I do differently. They have become habit to me now. When people come to my home, they often cannot tell which white dog is Treasure until I point her out to them. She fits right in with the family and is so comfortable in her home that it's not obvious that she's different.

Preparing for Your New Arrival!

Dog-proofing your home

It's important when bringing any new dog into the home, to take an inventory of anything that might be damaging to or become damaged by the new addition. Because you don't know this new dog very well, it's important to pick up and put away anything that may be chewed or eaten. Block off expensive antiques for a bit, put shoes in the closet, etc. Make sure any hazardous products and items are safely out of the dog's reach. There are many resources out there to give you ideas about what to look for when dog-proofing your home. The better you dog-proof, the easier your job will be once the dog comes home.

Once things are picked up and put away that need to be, you can focus on setting up your home for the safety of a visually-impaired dog. There are some special considerations to keep in mind. A visually-impaired dog will learn her way around your home and yard fairly quickly. Be aware of bushes and other low obstacles that may poke the dog's eyes if she runs into them. Putting a small garden fence around these places outside will allow your yard to still look attractive while keeping the dog safe. When you are setting up for safety, look at things from your dog's level. Sharp corners on furniture may be dangerous to your dog's eyes. Some people pad the corners of sharp furniture in the beginning until their b/d dog learns where the obstacles are. You can wrap corners with towels or bubble wrap in a pinch.

Any drop-offs need to be safely gated off. In-ground swimming pools, steep flights of steps, balconies, large holes in the yard – any of these can be dangerous to a dog that can't see properly. Some dogs may be able to see, but may still have difficulty with depth perception, also needing to be kept safe from drop-offs.

Make sure there are safety measures in place at all entryways. Gates should be secured outside and checked often. Think about guests coming and going, or children running in and out of doors, or even a delivery brought to the door. If a b/d dog sneaks out a door unnoticed, she could be long gone before anyone goes searching. Adding an extra gate at the door or on the porch in case the dog tries to slip out is a good safety measure. Never underestimate your dog's ability to squeeze through or into small spaces!

The home layout

Think about where you want your dog's things to be located. Especially in the beginning, you will want the dog's crate, bed and bowls to be kept in the same spots so she can find them easily. If you want to rearrange your furniture, do it before the dog arrives, so things can remain in place while the dog is getting used to its new home and routine.

One thing that can be helpful to b/d dogs is to place non-slip rugs at the various thresholds in your home. Your dog will learn these rugs as points on her mental map. Some places that rugs may be helpful are at the top and bottom of all stairs, and at the front and back doors to the house, or at least at the door that you will use to take your dog outside.

Outside, you can define areas in the yard by using a doormat by the door back into the house, and by using dog-safe mulch around trees so she will know she is approaching the tree and can turn or slow down. If you have a stone path or other landscaping objects in your yard, your dog will learn to use them to find her way around easily.

Using non-slip treads on any non-carpeted stairs will help your dog feel more secure. Another thing to consider about steps is that some steps are open on the sides. This openness can be scary to a dog that cannot see. You may consider adding a railing on sides that are open. If you have a smaller dog, make sure the slats on all railings are narrow enough that your dog can't fall through. She won't be able to see the drop-off on the other side.

Some tips to get you started

Some of these miscellaneous tips may help you prepare for your new dog's arrival, or in the early days as you are both getting used to each other.

Some people like to put a small bell on their b/d dog's collar so they know where the dog is. This can be very helpful, but just be aware that if the dog is sleeping, the bell won't be making any noise. And if your dog paces at night, the bell may keep you awake unless you remove it at bedtime. The jingling of dog tags can also let you know where your dog is.

Use large heavy ceramic bowls to reduce spills. Blind dogs often bump into the bowl or may even step in it as they are trying to find exactly where it is in space. They may know where the bowl is kept, but sometimes aiming for the opening is tricky. Also, putting a rug under the bowl that sticks out a bit allows the dog time to slow down before bumping into the bowl. Outside, a water bucket can have the handle clipped to a fence to keep it upright. Some people also find elevated bowls to be helpful in preventing messes.

Keep an ID tag attached to your dog's collar or harness at all times! It is also a good idea to get your dog micro-chipped, because collars and tags do sometimes fall off. This may be the only way your dog will be returned to you if it gets loose and someone finds it. I like to have a two-sided ID tag made with "Blind and Deaf" written on one side, and my information on the other.

I use ID tag covers around my dog's tags so they don't leave a ring of grey around her neck. She is white and the metal tags will leave a grey residue over time. You can find these online or make your own. Plastic tags may also cut down on the discoloration of the fur, but they are not as durable as metal tags.

Be aware that snow can cover scents, surfaces, and landmarks that your dog usually uses to get around in the yard. She may get lost in her own yard after a good snow. Keep key surfaces cleared off so she can smell and feel them easily. I have a wooden ramp that leads to the door to my house. In the winter, if I don't keep it cleared off, Treasure has a hard time finding the entrance to the ramp. She is used to feeling for the wooden surface with her feet.

A blinking tag or a glow-in-the-dark collar may help you keep track of your dog at night in the yard. If your dog sees flashes, a blinking tag may be confusing to her, but one that glows steadily may be ok. You'll just have to see what works best for your dog.

Dogs that have some vision may appreciate having a night light left on at bedtime. It may help lessen any anxiety. Some dogs have night blindness and as the environment gets darker, their ability to see declines. Having a bright porch light in the yard may also help give your dog confidence to go out on her own (always in a fenced area, of course). Flashing the porch light a couple times can become a signal that it's time to come inside.

Dogs losing their sight and hearing gradually may need more careful handling. Try very hard not to startle them. They may prefer to sleep in an open crate or a corner so they won't be snuck up on and caught off guard. Try not to move their things – bowls, beds, toys, crates – or your furniture. Try to keep their routine as consistent as possible so they know what to expect. Begin to introduce touch and other signals into their daily routine.

Use dog-safe sunscreen on your white dogs and don't let them stay outside during peak sunburn hours of the day. Your dog's eyes may be more sensitive to sunlight as well, causing her to squint and diminishing any vision that she normally has. Doggles can help protect your dog's eyes from bright sun, bushes and twigs, and flying bugs.

An angel vest can help if your dog is having trouble running into things. Give your dog some time to map things out first on her own. You will probably be surprised at how well she can get around on her own. But a dog losing her sight later in life may appreciate the help of the angel vest. The vest will be a new sensation for your dog, so use it for short periods of time at first when you are around to supervise. Do something fun with her while she wears the vest, so she learns to enjoy wearing it. Be aware that if you have other dogs, they may chew on or jump into the halo part of the vest when trying to play. Always supervise your dog while she's wearing the angel vest.

For a small dog, you may want to use pet steps to allow her to join you on the furniture. Place the steps so the sides are blocked by a wall or other barrier so she won't fall off the sides. Keep the steps in the same place all the time so she can find them to get on or off by herself.

Gear and Equipment

There is some equipment which you may find helpful when living with a b/d dog. I will try to give a brief description of them here to help you become better familiar with them. You can find more information in the resources section at the end of the book to help you find these gadgets.

Vibrating Collar:

Note that this is NOT a shock collar. Never use a shock collar on your b/d dog! A vibrating collar provides a gentle shaking sensation, similar to a pager or cell phone on a vibrate setting. Some people have had good luck using a vibrating collar with their dogs.

I don't have personal experience using a vibrating collar with a b/d dog. I did consider trying one, but decided against it. Most collars that I researched were large and bulky. My dogs are small and the bulky collars would not have been comfortable for them. My dogs also have lots of hair around their necks, which may inhibit the vibration signal. I did not want to keep their neck hair shaved short.

Some people do use a vibrating collar as a recall signal from a distance, or as a marker signal during training. If you were going to use the vibrating collar as a recall signal, it would work best if your dog was deaf but had some vision. You could give the collar signal, and when the dog looked around, you could wave her in toward you. With a b/d dog, it might not work as well because your dog wouldn't know where to turn to come to you after feeling the vibration.

I have heard that as a marker signal, a vibrating collar does have a delay between when you press the button and when the dog feels the vibration. So it may not be the best for training when you need to have precise timing.

Vibrating collars do have some limitations. They have a maximum distance, so if the dog is father away from you than that distance, the remote collar will not work. Batteries need to be checked and replaced often. Without batteries the collar will not work. They don't work that well with dogs with hairy necks unless you are willing to keep the hair trimmed short on a regular basis. And, collars can fall off.

If you choose to use a vibrating collar, research carefully to find the model that will work best for you. Choose a collar with only a vibration feature, NOT one with a shock option. It is too easy to push the wrong button and shock your dog.

Doggles:

Doggles are protective goggles made to fit a dog's head and stay in place. They can protect a dog's eyes from the damaging rays of the sun and also from punctures and scratches or other injuries. They come in many colors and sizes so your dog can make her own fashion statement. They are easily adjustable in size. Your dog will need to get used to wearing Doggles gradually. Have her wear them for short periods of time at first. Don't just put them on and let her struggle with them. When you put them on, let it be a fun time – pet her, play with her, feed her treats, feed her a meal, take her for a short walk – and distract her from wanting to rub them off. Take them off while she is calm and not fighting them. Gradually, work your way up to having her wear them for longer periods of time.

Canes for dogs:

Yes, there are various canes made to prevent your dog from bumping into obstacles! Basically, they stick out ahead of the dog's head so she will stop before hitting her face on things in her way. You can make something at home, or buy one already made. You can choose to make it as fashionable as you wish. Usually these do not protect your dog from being poked by branches and things that can easily poke past the cane. But they work well for preventing your dog from crashing into large obstacles in her path.

As with any equipment, get your dog used to these gradually. If she just stands in one place as if frozen, gently help her to move by scattering food near her. As she hunts for the food, she will begin to move and will see that it's safe to move while wearing something new. Be sure to supervise her while she is wearing any equipment. If she got stuck on something, she would probably panic. Also, other dogs may try to chew on or jump on top of the cane while they are trying to play.

Head halters and front-clip harnesses:

There are many brands of head halters available for dogs. Because the leash attaches near the head, these can be useful for guiding your b/d dog while on walks to prevent her from bumping into things. By steering your dog's head around obstacles, her body will follow easily. With a collar, some dogs may still bump their faces into objects while you try to stop them with the leash. Being able to stop the dog's head before it bumps into something can be helpful. Make sure you choose a style where the leash attaches under the dog's chin. There are some styles where the leash attaches behind the dog's head, which is not very useful for steering her head around an obstacle.

Dog harnesses designed for a leash to clip onto the front of the dog's chest can also be helpful for the same reasons. You can more easily control the front end of the dog, her speed and direction. Both of these pieces of equipment can help teach your dog not to pull on the leash as well. Be sure you learn how to fit the head halter or harness properly, and that you learn how to use it in the way it was intended.

Collars, harnesses, and leashes:

Take extra precautions when purchasing equipment for your b/d dog that she won't be able to back out of them if she is spooked by something. Regular buckle collars are great for keeping ID tags on your dog, but may not be the best option for walking your dog. I am especially aware of this since I live with shelties and whippets. Both breeds have very small narrow heads and are able to pull backwards and get their heads out of buckle collars if they are frightened.

For walking purposes or when going into public, my dogs wear properly-fitted martingale collars. These are collars that tighten when pulled, but they only tighten to a certain point. When properly fitted, they do not hurt the dog if pulled. If the dog should pull backwards against the leash, the martingale collar will close to form a very snug collar the exact size of the dog's neck up near its ears, preventing the dog from getting loose.

If you are concerned about the possibility of your dog getting loose, you can also use a leash with a clip on each end. One clip can be attached to a collar and one end to a harness, so you have an extra line of defense should your dog slip out of one. You can also use a double-ended leash with one end on the head halter and one end on the collar. Head halters can sometimes be easy for dogs to pull out of, so having the other end of the leash attached to the collar is a good safety measure.

Overall, every piece of equipment you use should be fitted properly to your individual dog, and you should know how to use it in the way it was intended to be used. Equipment can't keep your dog safe if it is not fitted well and used properly.

Thundershirt:

The Thundershirt is an amazing invention! It is useful in so many situations. The Thundershirt is a pressure wrap garment that helps to calm anxious dogs. It is easy to put on and take off and is washable. It even comes in cool colors!

Thundershirts are great for calming dogs during thunderstorms and other events that cause stress and anxiety, for dogs who get nervous visiting the vet or riding in the car, for new dogs that are unsettled, for dogs that spin, for dogs that get nervous in public or in certain situations like dog class or when guests come over, etc.

It's important to use the Thundershirt during times when your dog is calm also. If you only put the Thundershirt on your dog when something upsetting is going to happen, she will start to anticipate unpleasant things when the shirt is on. The goal is for the shirt to help her relax, so sometimes put it on her while she is already relaxing. The Thundershirt is also not meant to be put on the dog and left on for days at a time. The dog's body will begin to acclimate to the pressure and it won't be as comforting to her anymore. The Thundershirt can be used for several hours at a time if necessary, but should be used periodically and not constantly.

Puppy bumpers:

Puppy bumpers are made to keep small dogs safe from slipping through deck and balcony railings. It is made of a soft stuffed collar that sticks out away from your dog's neck and widens your dog's body space so she can't fit through the openings in the railing. They come in assorted colors and patterns.

You can also use mesh netting attached very securely to all railings to prevent your dog from sneaking through. Puppy bumpers might be a good thing to take with you when visiting other homes that don't have mesh on their railings.

Strollers and wagons:

These come in handy mostly for smaller b/d dogs. Small dogs can ride in a stroller in crowded public places to keep them up out of harm's way and to help them be more visible to people who may not be looking down. There are strollers created for dogs that often have a mesh panel that can be zipped closed to keep your dog inside the stroller. Some people also use a human baby stroller and just teach their dog not to jump out. A wagon can be used for multiple small dogs or a medium-sized dog. These are also very nice for elderly dogs that want to be included on outings, but may not be able to walk as far as they used to.

Making Introductions

Bringing your new b/d dog home

When you bring a new dog into your home, everything is brand new to her. Don't assume anything about your dog's past. Start with a clean slate. Your b/d dog may have come from a wonderful home where she was loved and included, or she may have come from a place where she wasn't. Either way, you will be trying to win the trust of a dog that has had her world turned upside-down, losing everything she's ever known up until this point.

It will take time, from weeks to months, for your dog to feel completely comfortable in her new home. She will need to learn her way around the house and yard, your routine, to trust in new family members and pets, and to begin to learn what is expected of her. Use gates to keep her in the same room as you, so you can provide supervision and so you can teach her great behavior habits right from the start. It will help your training go faster.

Stress levels may be high – yours and the dog's. Be understanding. Be patient. When you are frustrated, take some time for yourself. Make sure the dog is some place safe and take a break. If you don't, your frustration will continue to build and your dog will recognize that something is wrong, but won't know why. That will further increase her stress level. Practice stress relief techniques for yourself, your family, your existing pets, and the new dog, during this adjustment period. You may find it helpful to keep a little journal of your experiences with your new dog. Sometimes we don't notice the progress being made until we go back and remind ourselves how things started and how much we've accomplished.

Take it slow and allow the process to unfold as it will. Don't expect everything to happen all at once. If you are working on something and it's not going the way you had hoped, it's ok to stop. Just take a break and do something fun with your dog instead. Tomorrow is another day and often, when we take some time away from the situation, we can see how to do things differently the next time for better success. A relationship is a process that is constantly evolving and changing. What fun to see how it develops and where it takes you next. Enjoy the journey!

Introducing your dog to your home

When you get your new dog home, take the time to let her sniff the yard and do her business before going inside. Show her around the yard on leash, even if it is fenced. Go with her and help her explore safely. She may need to sniff around a lot before deciding to do her business. Remember, she is in a totally new area and she won't be able to gain information about where she is from looking around. She needs to explore by sniffing. Give her the time she needs to feel comfortable with the environment and do what she has to do.

When you show her around the house and yard for the first time, it's best to put any resident dogs into another area. Let the new dog focus on knowing where she is before she has to meet and greet the other dogs. She will smell their scents around as she is exploring, which will help when it's time for introductions.

Once she has taken care of her business outside, take her into the house. Again, keep her on leash and go with her to help steer her around the major obstacles. She will bump into some things in the beginning, but the leash will help you keep that to a minimum as she explores. Anything fragile or that can be easily tipped over should have already been put away or secured.

Expect that your dog will need to explore the same area many times. This is how she will begin to create a mental map of where everything is and which room leads to where. Keep her on leash for a while longer if you think she needs the extra help. Start to follow her and allow her to explore, but with you close by to intervene if necessary. Soon, you will be able to remove the leash, but don't be in too big of a hurry in the beginning.

Help her create a mental map

There are things you can do to assist your b/d dog with creating a mental map of your home and yard. Remember that this will take some time. If your home has many rooms, not only will your dog need to learn her way around each room and where the furniture is located, but she will need to learn the layout of how each room leads to the next, where the doors are to go outside, etc. How long this will take will vary with each individual dog.

Allow safe and supervised exploring, using a leash to help when needed or gently steering your dog by the collar if she's comfortable with that. She will need to spend a lot of time sniffing the ground and objects to gather information. It may be useful in the beginning to only allow exploring after your dog has done her business outside. With a new dog, it may be difficult to tell whether she is sniffing to explore or sniffing to find the right spot!

Begin to walk your dog along certain paths that she will use frequently. You can do this just as part of the daily routine. She will need to learn how to get from her crate or pen to the outside doors rather quickly for housetraining purposes. Always keep her crate or pen in the same place. This is very important in the beginning while she is creating a map. Later, if you need to change it, there will be an adjustment period, but she will already know the rest of the map, so she should be able to adjust with time. For right now, though, the more things you can keep in their place, the better.

She will also need to know how to get from various areas of the house to the outside door. Don't try to teach all these routes all at once, but in your day to day activities, wherever she is when it's time to go outside, take the time to walk her there in a fairly direct path and she will begin to learn.

By keeping things in the same place, you can also give your dog a reference point as to where she is. With a larger dog, this may not be as much of a consideration because she will normally walk to wherever she is going. With a small puppy or dog, however, there may be times when you are holding or carrying her with you. Try to set her down in an area where there is something familiar so she can get her bearings and figure out where she is and where she wants to go from there. You can put her down in or near a dog bed, her crate, near the food and water bowls, etc. Of course in the beginning, she will still be lost, but as she maps out the place, she will know exactly where you put her down and this will help her to feel secure.

Human family members

Even though your b/d dog won't be able to see her new human family members, she will be able to smell them and will feel vibrations as they move around. For some dogs, this may be confusing at first, as all the new people crowd around to welcome the new dog. Try having the people sit down on the floor and stay in one place. Allow your dog to sniff and meet each person one at a time. Treats can help to begin to create a positive association right away between each person's scent and good things.

It is especially important to allow the new dog to approach each person on her own if she is shy or hesitant at all. Grabbing at her may make her insecurity worse. Let a shy dog make the decision to come to you when she feels comfortable. If she is friendly and interested, reaching out to touch her softly is a great way to start the bonding process. Most dogs don't like to be suddenly touched on top of their heads, especially dogs that can't see the hand coming toward them. Start touching gently on the dog's chest or shoulder and then gradually move your hand from there if she is accepting.

Animal family members

When introducing your b/d dog to other household animals, remember to take safety precautions. With cats, be very aware of their claws. A b/d dog cannot see the cat taking a swipe at her in order to move backward and her eyes may get scratched. Supervise closely and keep the new dog on a leash at first until you know how she will react. She may decide to chase or try to grab your cat!

If you have small animals in your home, again, introduce your b/d dog to them carefully, keeping in mind that small animals are natural prey to dogs. Keep the small animal caged and have your dog on a leash so you can prevent any incidents.

When introducing dogs to each other, it is best to do introductions on a neutral territory if possible. Perhaps you can take the resident dog for a walk and meet the new dog at a park or even out in the front yard if he doesn't spend a lot of time there. Some dogs get very territorial with a new dog on their property, so by going someplace neutral, you can remove that from the equation.

Have both dogs on leash with two separate handlers if possible. Try to keep both dogs' leashes loose. A tight leash puts a dog on guard and increases any tension already present from meeting a new dog. Dogs must smell each other in very private places when getting to know each other. They will most likely begin to circle around each other while they are sniffing. This means that the people handling the leashes must also move in order to follow their dog and not allow leashes to tangle. After a few seconds of sniffing, move the dogs apart for a few moments. This prevents things from getting too intense too quickly. After a minute, allow another interaction, again, keeping leashes loose and following dogs to prevent tangling.

If you are alone and trying to introduce two dogs, or, if going to a neutral area is not possible, you can utilize tools such as gates or ex pens to help you manage both dogs until you are sure they are ok with each other. Put the new dog in the gated area and bring the resident dog to sniff and say hello. Keep the resident dog on leash. Allow a few seconds of sniffing and then move him away for a break. Repeat a minute or so later. Continue this pattern while both dogs get used to each other. If you have more than one resident dog, introduce them each individually, not as a group.

If things go well through the gate, you can move the introduction outside to the yard or a place where there is a bit more room. Again, only bring out one resident dog at a time. If you are alone and don't have someone to help you, let the new dog outside first (into a securely fenced area), and then bring the resident dog out on a leash so you can control the interaction. If you can have two people during this stage, one to handle each dog, it makes things easier. Proceed as above, allowing short periods of sniffing.

If the dogs want to play, you can drop the leashes (if it is a safe area to do so) and allow some interaction. If either of the dogs seems stressed, move them apart and take another break. It may take them some time to begin to like each other. Just like with people, some hit it off right away and other relationships take time to develop. If things are going well with all the introductions, you can then introduce having two of the resident dogs with the new dog. If you have more than two resident dogs, just add dogs one at a time and slowly.

This may be a one-day process, or you may need to keep dogs separated as you integrate the whole group over several days. Either way is normal and you should not be upset if it takes a little more time. Always supervise any pets together with a new dog for an extended adjustment period even if you think they are getting along fine. Always be ready to intervene!

Bonding

This seems to be a major concern with people that I counsel. They are concerned about how they will bond with a blind and deaf dog. The biggest consideration when bonding with any dog is to establish trust! With a b/d dog, that is no different. You are your dog's eyes and ears, and you must be sure she stays safe. She needs to have every confidence that you will not put her in danger. And, danger is not your perception of danger – it is her perception of it. So anything that scares or confuses her, in her mind, is dangerous.

Routines can help to develop trust because they allow your dog to relax and know what is coming next in her day. She will learn that you will take care of her needs. In the beginning, sticking to a set routine will help your dog be more relaxed and learn to trust that you will make sure she has everything she needs. Also, a routine is important for housetraining!

It takes time to build up a level of trust. Each dog is different and each relationship develops at a different rate. Watch out for her. Trust is a fragile thing.

There are two sides to every bond. For your dog to bond with you, you need to begin establishing trust right away. Dogs also bond with those that care for them, so treats and feeding meals can be a good first step in the bonding process if your dog is food motivated. Touch can also be a huge component in building a bond. Touch will become a very important part of your b/d dog's life.

Use lots of gentle and soothing touch. Handle her all over if she is comfortable with that, always gently, never forcing beyond her comfort level or she will struggle to avoid your touch instead of enjoying it. If there are places that your dog doesn't want you to touch her, stick with places she likes to be touched. Later on, after you have developed trust and a bond, you can work on teaching her to allow touch everywhere.

Spend time being close to your dog. Treasure enjoys being held close to my chest and throat while I sing or hum to her. She can feel the soothing vibrations and my breathing. She can tell that I am calm and it helps to create a sense of calm in her as well. Some dogs enjoy being held and rocked gently. They are calmed by the slow repetitive movements and being close to your body.

For you to bond with your new dog, spend time with her. Watch her. Appreciate how she can know where she is in a dark and silent world. Memorize all the little details about her. Just sit with her, touch her, enjoy her. Don't get so caught up in making everything work right away that you lose sight of the fact that you have this marvelous creature in your life.

Bringing a blind and deaf dog into your life can seem overwhelming and frustrating at times. In fact, sometimes it seems that way most of the time in the beginning. Take a break when you need to. Put your dog some place safe with something to keep her occupied and go do something to help yourself relax. Your feelings are normal. Each day it will get easier if you are nice to yourself. Stop and just enjoy watching her putter around the yard in the sunshine. No need to try to accomplish anything, just enjoy her.

And remember that each relationship is different. Each one happens in its own time. You can't rush it. It will develop as you learn to appreciate each other. Enjoy the process.

Day to Day Stuff

Housetraining

Any new dog needs to be set up on a housetraining regimen right away. Even an adult dog that may have been well-trained to go outside at another house would benefit from a set routine and supervision for a while in a new home. The stress of moving to a new home can lead to drinking more water and more frequent urges to go outside or to the urge to urine mark the new environment. Just because a dog has been housetrained in one home, does not mean that will transfer to other homes. Close supervision in the beginning will help prevent accidents.

Here are some tips to set you and your new dog up for success:

While allowing free access to fresh drinking water is important, do not let her gulp a lot of water before your bedtime. If it's hot or your dog is thirsty, try giving her a couple ice cubes to lick, or a few sips of water at a time. Remember that what goes in, must come out. So not giving your dog a lot of water before it goes to bed will help you to be able to sleep through the night undisturbed!

It is easiest to housetrain your dog if you create a routine. Always take your dog outside first thing in the morning when she wakes up. A puppy won't be able to hold it, so carry her outside quickly! Take her out after every meal or as soon as she has finished an active playtime. Also, most dogs need to go outside after a long nap. Any time you take your dog out of her crate or from confinement, she should make a trip outside. Of course, anytime you see your dog sniffing or circling suspiciously, take her outside as well. Puppies will need to go more often than adult dogs, but it won't hurt an adult dog to be taken out more frequently in the beginning. You will start to learn her routine and when she needs to go and can then begin to take her out less frequently. It's always better to take the dog out more often in the beginning than to have accidents in the house.

When you take your dog outside, it may be easier in the beginning to always take her to the same spot in the yard so she will smell her scent there and it will be a familiar potty spot for her. The same is true if you have a spot where your other dogs do their business. She will smell their smells there and know what that area is for. If you have other dogs outside with you, often if one dog goes, another dog will also go in that same general area. If one of your other dogs goes, take the new dog over to that area to sniff and she may decide to go as well.

Choose a potty touch cue to use with your dog and use it as soon as you get to the potty area of the yard with your dog. Soon, she will start to associate that touch cue with doing her business and you will find that you can get her to go quickly by using the cue. Treasure's potty cue is three quick taps on the top of her tail.

It is important to praise your dog for doing her business outside where you want her to go. With a b/d dog, you will need to stand close enough to your dog that you can pet her as she is going. Using a leash, even in a fenced yard, will make it easier to be close to her at the right time. Pet gently, because if you are too enthusiastic, you may distract her and stop her before she's completely finished. If you find that your dog is very distracted by the petting during her business, try to pet immediately as she is finishing. If you wait for her to walk away from the spot, she may not make the association between the petting and doing her business.

When you are in the house, keep your dog within your sight. Know where she is and what she is doing. If you can't supervise closely, confine your dog to a smaller area to prevent mistakes. Dogs will usually try to keep a smaller area clean. A crate or ex pen works well for this, or confine your dog to a smaller dog-proof room. If the area is too big, your dog may still have accidents, so the smaller the area, the better.

If your dog does have an accident, never try to correct or punish her after the fact. She probably won't associate you being upset with something that she did a while ago. If you catch her in the act, get to her quickly and distract her with a quick touch. Get her very quickly outside and give her time to finish outside so you can pet and reward her for going in the right place. Always clean up accidents with products made specifically for cleaning up dog accidents! Other cleaners may just cover up the odor, but a dog's nose will still be able to detect the scent of a previous accident. It may also help to anchor a paper towel outside that you used to clean up an indoor accident. This will put the scent in the proper place.

Vow to watch your dog more closely and prevent any future accidents. If you aren't supervising and your dog has frequent accidents, she is just rehearsing a behavior that you don't want her to do, and it will become habit.

Crate training

It's important not to just put a new dog into a crate and close the door unless you know for sure that she is comfortable being crated. While this is true for any dog, it seems to be especially true for b/d dogs. A dog that can see or hear would still be able to gather clues from her environment while crated that you are nearby. A b/d dog has no clue what has happened when she suddenly finds herself stuck in a box that she can't get free from. She is likely to panic.

Teaching your dog to accept being in a crate is an important lesson for her to learn. Even if you don't plan to use a crate in your dog's day-to-day life, there may be times when you will need to use one. Crates are handy for safety while traveling in the car and for staying in new places like hotels. A crate can become her home away from home – a place that she knows is her own. If your dog ever needs to stay at the vet's office for a procedure, she may find herself in a small cage similar to a crate. If she is not used to staying calm while in a crate, she may be very stressed and panicked while at the vet's office, which will delay her recovery. Many grooming shops also use crates for dogs that are waiting to be picked up.

You can keep an open crate inside the pen or confinement area for your dog. Be sure to remove or secure the door of the crate so it can't accidently close, trapping your dog inside. Putting a bed inside the crate may encourage your dog to want to check it out. Many dogs like to have a small cozy place to sleep. Deaf and b/d dogs tend to like sleeping in an area that is out of the general path so they won't be startled as frequently. A crate with the door always open can provide that for them.

Of course, in order for a crate to become useful to you, you must be able to close the door with your dog inside. This will require some training time. Sit on the floor with an open crate and your dog. Put any other dogs in a different part of the house for this. Have some very tasty treats with you. With the crate door removed or secured open, put a treat on the floor near the doorway of the crate. Don't force your dog; just let her smell the treat as you put it on the floor. Pet her if she eats it and replace it with another treat in the same spot on the floor. Continue feeding her treats quickly until she's eaten about 5 – 6 from the floor just outside the crate.

Then put the treat just inside the doorway of the crate. With a metal crate, this will mean your dog must reach her neck in over the lip or that she must step over the lip at the bottom of the door. This can be confusing to some dogs, so if you need to, hold the treat in your hand and help her to stretch her neck for the treat a little more each time. Reward often to keep it fun for her and to prevent her from worrying. With a plastic crate, you can place the food on top of the lip at the bottom of the door where there is a flat ledge.

As your dog becomes more comfortable, gradually move the treat back farther and farther into the crate, or make a small trail of treats close together for her to follow. Never try to force her into the crate or you will undo the work you have already done. Don't try to close the crate door at this point.

It may take many sessions for your dog to be comfortable entering the crate by herself. Be patient. Once she's comfortable, begin to feed her meals to her inside the open crate. At first, just inside the door, so she can eat with her body outside of the crate if she wants to. Then gradually move the bowl farther and farther back until she is eating with her entire body in the crate. She may decide to eat a bite and then come out of the crate, go back in for another bite, etc. That's fine at this stage. When she begins to feel comfortable enough to stay inside the crate for her entire meal, you can then move on to the next step.

Now, once your dog is inside the crate and begins eating, close the crate door but don't latch it. Stay very close by and as soon as she is finished and tries to come out of the crate, open the door for her and let her out. Don't try to make her stay inside at this point. Let her notice the door is closed, and then immediately open it and let her out.

After doing this for a few meals, latch the crate door as she starts eating. Stay right next to the crate. When she tries to come out, pause for only a few seconds and then let her out while she is still calm and quiet. Don't give her time to get upset. You want being in the crate to always be a good thing for her.

Gradually, over time, you will be able to build up the time that she is in the crate. Go slowly. It only takes one bad experience for her to decide that she doesn't like the crate! And it will take a longer time for you to un-teach that reaction.

There are some things you can do at this stage to make crating easier for your dog. Choose times when your dog is tired and relaxed to put her in the crate. This will encourage her to be calm in the crate. Put her in the crate with food toys to keep her occupied and a bone to chew. See the enrichment section for more about food toys.

Your b/d dog is very aware of vibrations, smells, and air currents around her. These are ways she gets information about what's going on in her environment. Something as routine as the heat or air conditioning coming on, or another dog walking past or sniffing her crate, may get her excited. Covering the crate with a light sheet may help to reduce distractions and keep your dog calmer while she's in the crate. If your dog can see shadows and changes in light, covering the crate may minimize her becoming excited over those things as well. Pulling drapes or a shade closed may also help with this.

Dogs that can hear may appreciate soft music playing. I have placed a radio on top of my dog's plastic crate so she could feel the vibrations. I don't know for sure that this was helpful, but it didn't hurt anything and kept my other dogs that could hear calmer around her, which in turn helped her to be calmer. If your dog is bothered by the vibrations of the music, do not put the radio on top of her crate because the crate will then vibrate, increasing her stress.

Leaving something with your scent on it for your dog may be soothing. A piece of worn clothing or your shoes left just outside the crate door may help. As you bond, your scent will be associated with calm and petting and may help her to remain calmer with that part of your presence near. If you are sure your dog won't eat the article of clothing, you can put it inside the crate with her to snuggle up with.

It is a good idea to try to avoid rewarding poor crate behavior by letting your dog out. Some dogs will learn that the poor behavior will cause you to come let them out, and they will become obnoxious in the crate. If your dog is genuinely distressed in the crate and it is getting worse, try to distract her first by putting your finger through the bars, or with a gentle tap on the crate. This MUST be done gently, not as a correction or in anger. B/d dogs are very aware of vibrations, so it won't take much to get her attention. The instant she stops barking or trying to get out, open the door to let her out. In this instance, you would be rewarding that calm and quiet moment by letting her out. With consistency, she will learn that calm and quiet behavior gets her let out.

If your dog is distressed in the crate, it means that you need to go back a few steps and review your training to create a positive feeling about the crate for your dog. A dog that is barking and excited because you've come back into the room is not necessarily distressed. But still, distract her for a moment and then reward that moment of desired behavior by letting her out. Puppies will bark or whine and get restless if they need to potty while in the crate. Again, distract with a little tap on the crate or stick your fingers through the bars for her to smell. Let her out quickly when she's calm and get her outside.

Just a note here: some dogs do better with a larger crate or an ex pen where they are less confined and have more room to move around. If your dog is having a hard time getting used to a smaller crate, you may want to try this option. Leaving a distressed dog in a crate to get used to it, rarely works, and will usually create more anxiety for your dog surrounding the crate, which can lead to other unwanted behaviors such as soiling the crate.

Day vs. night

If your b/d dog is unable to distinguish between light and dark, it may be challenging to help her tell the difference between day and night. This can make it challenging for you to get enough sleep on a schedule. Keeping a bedtime routine can be helpful. Create as many clear cues as possible that it is bedtime and only use them when you want her to let you sleep all night. Here are some ideas that may be helpful.

It may be helpful to create certain rules that pertain to night time only. If you enjoy having your dog share the bed with you, it may be a good idea to keep the bed off limits to her unless it is time to actually go to sleep for the night. Even if you don't want your dog on the bed with you, you can keep the bedroom off limits until bedtime. Then the bedroom itself will become a cue that it's time for sleeping.

I would be careful about using a crate or an ex pen as a cue for it being night time because there may be other times that you will need to utilize a crate or pen. If you choose to use this as a cue, it may never be as clear to your dog as if you used cues that are only used at night time.

You can reserve a special blanket or dog bed for your dog to only use at night. It will need to be picked up during the day, or have access to it restricted in some way. If used consistently, your dog will learn that this bed means that it is time to sleep. A relaxing scent such as lavender or other essential oils can be placed on her bed. The scent will also become a cue. Be careful that the smell has a chance to air out slightly so that your dog is not overwhelmed by the smell. Only use this scent at bedtime. If you need a way to confine your dog at night, the special bed can be put into an ex pen only at bedtime, or you can use a short tether near your bed to keep the dog on her bed.

Keeping your b/d dog busy during the day with enrichment games and activities will help her to begin to differentiate between day activities and sleeping at night. It will also help to tire out her body and mind so she is more likely to sleep at bedtime. A nice bodywork (calm petting, massage, Healing Touch for Animals®, etc.) session before bedtime will help your dog to relax and calm down.

If your dog wakes you in the middle of the night and you think she needs to go outside, keep it very quick and business-like. Keep any touching and interaction to a minimum. Don't let her loose in the yard to run and explore. Don't involve the other dogs. Make it a very quick and boring trip outside on leash, stand still and wait for her to potty (no walking and sniffing), no treats or playtime, and right back to bed. I don't even pet and praise the potty during the night. If you make getting up in the middle of the night fun for your dog and let her do things that she enjoys, she will continue to wake you up at night. Keep it boring at night and exciting and fun during the day and she will learn the routine.

Some dogs enjoy a large stuffed animal to snuggle with at night so they don't feel so alone. Puppies especially are used to snuggling with their mom and littermates and a large stuffed toy or pillow will give them a sense of security. An old-style ticking clock placed in the bed may also help sooth puppy to sleep. It will provide a rhythmic vibration throughout the night. If you remove it during the day, you can then use it as a cue to your dog that it is nighttime.

Dogs with some vision, but that can only see close up, may like to have you nearby. Put her bed or pen by your bed so you can put your fingers in to reassure her if she wakes up. A nightlight may help her not be so anxious by allowing her to see somewhat.

Mealtimes

There are a couple things to consider when feeding your b/d dog. If you have multiple dogs in your home, it is important to feed the b/d dog separate from the other dogs. The other dogs may be able to steal her food because she can't see them coming. She will not get enough food for herself, and she may learn to become protective of her food, which is not a good thing. You can feed her in a crate or behind a gate or in another room. This way she won't be worried that her food will be stolen.

It is important to play food bowl games with your dog if she is a puppy. You can play these at mealtimes, or you can play them anytime. Only play food bowl games with one dog at a time. The idea is to create calm and positive associations around the food bowl, not to create competition and resource guarding. Some of these instructions assume that your dog may have some vision. It is important to know what to look for with dogs that may have some vision, because they may react sooner or differently than dogs without. If your dog has no vision, you can adapt the instructions accordingly.

Don't start playing food bowl games until your dog has had a few weeks to settle into your home. A dog in a new home will be stressed and will be more likely to be insecure about certain resources, such as her food bowl. Give her time to adjust to the new house, and the new people in that house, before you begin playing food bowl games.

If your dog is an older puppy or an adult, playing food bowl games can be a good exercise if she does not try to guard her bowl. Proceed with caution when working with an older dog until you know her normal behavior around her food. Older dogs may have already learned to protect their food and the situation may require that you work with a professional trainer to remedy it. Do not punish your dog for trying to protect her food. This could make the situation worse, and you could be injured. This is an issue that will require gradual desensitization and training to resolve. Seek a professional's help.

Some signs that a dog is becoming worried around her food bowl include: eating faster as approached, her body posture flattening towards the ground and usually over the bowl, her head and body will block the opening of the bowl to limit others' access, the hair on her neck, shoulders and back standing on end (raised hackles), growling or snapping, lifting her lips, or she may freeze, stop eating and stare hard from the side of her eyes. If you feel in your gut that your dog might react, even if she is not showing any of these signs, respect that feeling and stay a safe distance away.

If your new dog already shows signs of protecting her food, start slowly with this process. Begin by just staying with your dog while she eats. Stay a safe distance away in the same room with her until she is finished eating. Just ignore her. She will know that you are there. If you ignore her, she will begin to relax and not worry about what might happen. Stay at that same distance for many meals until you see her beginning to relax in your presence. Make sure you stay in the area the whole time she is eating. If you show up in the middle, you may startle and worry her.

Gradually move closer during her meals. This is a gradual process. Don't rush it. You need to build her trust in you that you will not steal her food. This process should be done away from other household animals and children for everyone's safety. As you get closer to your dog, remain standing instead of sitting or stooping. This allows you to make a quick retreat if you need to protect yourself. If at any time, you are afraid or unsure, please seek the help of a professional trainer who has experience with these types of resource guarding behaviors.

To begin food bowl games:

Stand near your puppy for these games. With an empty food bowl, put a bit of very special food in the bowl. This is the time to check your refrigerator for food that your dog will love! Put a small bit in the empty bowl right in front of your dog and put the bowl down for her to eat. When she is finished drop another goodie in the bowl while it is on the floor. Do this 5-10 times and then stand up and walk away. Leave the bowl on the floor with your dog. She will eventually notice that there are no more goodies coming and will walk away. Once she leaves the bowl, you can pick it up and put it away. You can play this game for a few days and then move on to the next game. For a dog that is worried around her food bowl, it won't hurt to play this game for several weeks to build up a solid foundation before moving on.

After your dog is familiar with the first food bowl game, you can begin to add variations. Now you can begin to drop the next goodie while she is still eating the first one. This will require that you bend over and extend your reach just a bit in order to aim the second goodie into the bowl around your dog's head. Do not do this unless you feel comfortable with how your dog will react. When this is going well, begin by putting a bowl down that has a small handful of your dog's regular meal in it. As she is eating, drop in a few extra goodies. Don't progress unless you feel completely safe and comfortable with this step.

The next game is that you hold the food bowl while your dog eats. Begin with an empty bowl and hold it near your dog as you put a special goodie in it. Hold the bowl slightly below her mouth level so she can eat it, but don't let go of the bowl. She will smell that your hand is there near where she is eating. Wait until she is finished and then add another goodie. This is similar to the first game but you continue to hold the bowl throughout the whole process.

Now begin with a small handful of your dog's usual meal already in the bowl. Hold the bowl in your hand the whole time. While she is eating, add a special goodie to the bowl. You can play this game once or for her whole meal, adding a handful of the regular meal at a time and adding a goodie as she is eating each handful. By holding the bowl, you are teaching her that you can be close to her while she eats. Don't move on until she is completely comfortable with eating while you hold the bowl. Make sure you are holding the bowl for the entire time. Eventually you should be able to hold the bowl while your dog eats her entire meal.

When you reach this point, you may begin to occasionally pull the bowl up and away from your dog while she is eating, quickly pop a special goodie in the bowl, and then quickly return the bowl to her for her to finish the meal. Only remove the bowl once, and don't play this game a lot. Your dog should not have to be worried about her meal disappearing or being interrupted. Even if she allows you to do it, it will add stress to her mealtimes never knowing when her meal might be taken away. Practice this sparingly, and always add a very special treat to her bowl when you do.

It is important to reinforce food bowl manners that you like periodically throughout your dog's life. Every now and then walk up to your dog while she is eating and drop extra goodies into her dish if she remains calm and relaxed. If you begin to see signs of her worrying or protecting her food, pay attention to those signs and realize that you need to play a few more food bowl games or call in a professional trainer to help.

It is always important to give your dog a quiet and safe place to eat, where she doesn't feel that she has to be constantly on guard. Keep other pets and children away during mealtimes. With puppies, play lots of food bowl games to teach appropriate manners from the start. With new adult dogs, proceed with caution. You don't know what manners they have already learned or not learned. Go slowly.

Spinning

Spinning behavior can be seen more frequently in some breeds than in others. Shelties and some other herding breeds, and some toy breeds, are often spinners. I have seen dogs that have been confined to small spaces that have learned the pattern of spinning, usually only in one direction, as that was their pattern in the small space they were in. Dogs develop muscle memory and habits just like we do.

Spinning can also be a way for the dog to self-stimulate. If the dog is bored and starts to spin, her adrenaline starts to flow from the exciting activity. Dogs do get sort of addicted to things that make them feel better (like spinning) and will continue to do it over and over again.

Because spinning can quickly become a habit, it's not something that you should allow your dog to do continuously. Some dogs spin over and over again in a crate. If that's the case with your dog, try using a larger pen or a small room when you need to confine her, or use a seatbelt instead of a crate in the car. If you notice your dog aimlessly spinning at other times, distract her and give her something else to do. Treasure did a lot of spinning when I first brought her home. Some, no doubt, was linked to anxiety. As she got settled in and knew what to expect, the spinning decreased.

I found that a Thundershirt worked very well to stop the spinning. A Thundershirt is a pressure wrap that can help to calm anxious dogs. You can also use lots of enrichment activities to help distract your dog from spinning.

It's not the end of the world if your dog spins. Some spinning may just be how your dog expresses her excitement at the prospect of a meal, a walk, or a favorite game. Continuous spinning can be an issue, however, and when your dog gets into this pattern, it's best to give her something else to do or try a pressure wrap like the Thundershirt. In rare situations, dogs have been medicated through a prescription to stop compulsive spinning.

Car travel

If you have the opportunity to get your dog used to your car gradually before her first ride, that is ideal. Let her smell the car as you approach it and prevent her from bumping into it if you can. Help her into the car with it turned off first. Sit with her and give her a few treats if she will eat them. Let her sniff around. Help her into her crate or the spot where she will be riding and give her lots of attention while she is there. If she will be wearing a seatbelt, go ahead and hook her up for just a brief moment while you feed treats. Then unhook her. Don't let her get the feeling of being trapped. If she will be riding in a crate, feed her a treat and close the door while she is chewing. Then let her out again. Do this many times.

I prefer having my b/d dog in a crate when traveling because it gives me peace of mind that she is safe. Seatbelts are helpful, but a blind dog still will not be able to see items that may shift toward her if I have to stop suddenly. A crate will prevent anything from hitting her. If you choose to use a seatbelt, be certain that she cannot slip or flip off of the seat if you stop short.

You can begin to use the car touch cue with your dog from the start, and she will begin to learn what it means by association. Give the touch cue right before you help her into the car. If you are consistent, she will learn that when she feels that touch cue, she will then be getting into the car.

During your next session, have the car running while you help her in and into her riding spot. Spend more time with her hooked into her spot or in her crate. If you have someone to help you, have that person drive a short ride around the block while you sit in the back near your dog. You may need to interact with her a lot at first to keep her comfortable, but try to reduce the amount of interacting you do with her over future drives. You will one day want to take her some place when you are driving and no one is sitting near her.

Most of us do not have the luxury of getting our dog used to the car before needing to transport her home. Give her a few moments to sniff around in the car and in her spot before hooking her into place or putting her in the crate. Leave her with a few treats and a bone to chew. DAP (dog-appeasing pheromone) spray on a towel or bed in the crate or on the seat may help her to be calmer on her first trip. If she's very upset, a Thundershirt can also assist with calming. Be aware that she may get carsick, so using towels on the seat will help keep clean up simpler.

Walks

While out on walks, you will need to guide your dog around trees and other objects in her path. At first, this will take much concentration on your part, because these are not normally things you consciously watch out for. You will need to protect your dog from bumping into people, dogs, poles, hydrants, signs, anything and everything! You will also need to warn your dog of drop-offs and step-ups, like curbs or holes in the sidewalk. People walking will not necessarily go around your dog, as they won't know she can't see, so you will need to be careful to steer her safely out of the way.

People you meet may not understand why your dog is not responding to them the way other dogs might. Getting or making a dog jacket or bandana that explains that your dog is blind and deaf can help people be more understanding. Always be ready to jump in and assist them with saying hello to your dog. A sudden unexpected touch will startle your dog. If you see someone reaching out to touch your dog, reach your hand out first to let your dog smell and feel that someone will be touching her.

Socialization

Socialization is about creating positive associations for your dog about people, places, and things that she will come in contact with throughout her life with you. It is important that all exposures are positive for your dog. Once a fear is formed, it is very hard to extinguish.

It's important that you protect your b/d dog from anything that can physically hurt her or scare her, like obstacles, drop offs, or things that may hit her from overhead. She cannot see and prepare herself for dogs and people approaching, things falling or being thrown in her direction, etc. You must always be aware of the environment and what is happening to and around your dog. She relies on you to protect her.

Be aware of what signs of stress your dog may exhibit if she is unsure about something that is going on. These are signs that you are pushing too fast and that it is not a positive experience for your dog. If you see signs of stress, back off a bit and approach more gradually, making it a more positive experience for your dog.

Some signs of stress you may see while you are out and about are hard panting when your dog is not overly hot, sweaty paw prints on sidewalks and slick floors, spinning, grabbing the leash or hands in her mouth, grabbing food harshly, getting hyper, getting very quiet, hiding behind you, trying to leave, getting lower to the ground, or moving slower. See the signs of stress list that follows for more behaviors to watch for.

Food is a great way to create positive associations. Use and always carry the very favorite food treats when you are out and about with your dog. Associate new people with great food by feeding your dog while other people approach and pet your dog. Let your dog smell the person first and choose to approach, then feed small bits of treats while the person pets gently. Feed for as long as the person is petting.

When using food to help your dog feel positively about certain people or things, don't wait to feed her until she acts a certain way. Just feed for the sake of feeding, no matter how she is behaving. Feeding her if she is fearful will not make the fear worse. If she is too fearful or stressed, she probably won't eat anyway, which is fine. Just remove her from the situation until she calms down.

You can use bits of food to help your dog approach new objects and to walk on new surfaces to make sure her first association is a good one. Be sure to sprinkle some food near your dog and then put more closer to the surface so your dog can choose to go closer as she is comfortable. Never force your dog if she is scared, or you will make the fear worse. Using food to lure your dog closer may work with some dogs, but with others it may increase their worry about the situation. It's important if you want to use food to entice your dog into a situation, that you scatter the food and then let it be your dog's decision to proceed. This will keep the situation positive for her. If you are scattering food near an object, be careful that she will not bump into the item and get hurt.

It is extremely important to socialize puppies every day. The most crucial time for exposing puppies to our world is up until 4-5 months of age. Learning during this time will tend to be permanent and happens much faster than it will later. The more you can expose a puppy to in this time frame, the better, but only if all exposure is positive. Puppies will also learn very quickly to fear new things if they are pushed past their comfort levels. They must be able to make choices to approach when they are feeling comfortable. Never try to force them.

If they are feeling scared and you force them to approach, they will only become more afraid. If they are feeling a bit scared and you allow them to back off and reconsider the situation, they may then decide to approach once they calm down and realize there is nothing to fear.

It is important to continue socialization long after the 5-month mark, however. Dogs that don't get out and about much will tend to be more timid and anxious than those that get out and experience a lot of new people and things. Socialization is also a great way to tire out your dog. All the new smells and experiences are good mental stimulation for your dog and will tire her out.

With puppies and smaller dogs, you can carry them into new situations and let them become accustomed to the new smells and sensations from the security of your arms. Once they are relaxed, you can then put them down to explore if the situation is safe. It's not important that your dog be happy about everything she encounters. If she's worried about something, that's ok, but you need to allow her the decision to leave. Don't force her to stay. Try again later or even another day, and she may be ready to confront it then.

Socialization is about positive exposures, not forcing everything to be ok. Your job is to expose your dog to new things and to watch to make sure she is not becoming overly upset in the situation. Make every new thing a wonderful party if you can!

Stress in dogs

Dogs experience stress, just like we do. Not all stress is unpleasant, of course, but for the discussion in this book, let's assume that we are discussing unpleasant stress for your dog. Stress is a physiological reaction to something in the environment. It causes very real changes in your dog's body chemistry.

Stress is a fact of life we must all learn to deal with in appropriate ways. It is not the circumstances in life that are stressful by themselves, but it is our (and our dog's) perception of those circumstances that causes stress. Every person and every dog do not react in the same manner to the same situation. So, what might seem stressful to one, may not to another.

What situations might create a stress reaction for your dog? Being in a new environment or situation, being confused about what is expected of her or of how to react, anything that scares her, being in crowded places with very little personal space, having new people or animals enter her home, changes in known routines, being left alone, etc. These are only a few.

As you get to know your dog better, you will begin to know what types of situations are stressful for her. The important thing is to learn to recognize signs of stress in your dog so you will know when to step in and help her.

Dogs as a species show some of the same signs of stress, but individual dogs also show stress in their own ways. It's important to learn about these stress signals in dogs, but also to observe your own dog for behaviors that are different from her regular behavior. These might be signals that she is getting stressed as well.

Some signs of stress in dogs include:

Your dog may become more active, moving faster, pacing, or just acting like she can't sit still. Or she may become very still and seem distant or shut down, seeming to ignore things going on around her. She may even freeze in place and refuse to move at all.

She may back away or turn away from the situation. This may be very obvious, or it may just be that she averts her eyes or turns her head away very slightly. You may see her crouching down closer to the ground or cowering. Even a slight lowering of her body toward the ground can signal uncertainty and stress.

Dogs that are stressed may refuse to eat or drink. Sometimes dogs that travel, or are boarded, will not eat or drink normally due to the stress of being someplace new. In a new situation, you may find your dog won't eat treats that she normally would eat. This is due to being stressed. That being said, some dogs drink more when they are stressed, and some dogs will eat even when they are stressed, but they will start to chomp harder for the treats.

While some yawning is just a symptom of a sleepy dog, a big exaggerated yawn is a symptom of stress. Your dog may yawn at times other than nap times and will usually yawn frequently if she is stressed.

Panting heavily when she has not been exercising hard is a sign of stress. Her mouth may be dry, or it may be excessively wet with drool. Diarrhea and urine marking may be signs of stress.

If your dog is licking her lips with very quick and small movements, she is probably stressed. This one is easy to miss because the movement is so quick it's hard to see. Trembling can be a sign of stress, but it can also be a sign that the dog is cold or in pain. Whining and barking excessively is a sign of stress.

Chewing and mouthing behavior may increase when your dog is stressed. She may chew more when left alone if she is stressed. She may put her mouth on skin, clothing, her leash, etc., when she is stressed. Mouthing is normal in puppies, but you will notice if the puppy gets stressed the mouthing will escalate.

Any time your dog is trying to hide behind you or a barrier, she is stressed and wants to leave the situation. Shaking off her whole body as if she just had a bath is a sign of stress. You may see this after a stressful event, or you may see it repeatedly if the stressful situation continues. If you see wet paw prints on a surface when your dog has not just walked through something wet, she is stressed. Dogs sweat through their paw pads, so this is more obvious when they are stressed.

A dog that doesn't respond to known cues may be stressed. When a dog is stressed, she can't learn easily or think clearly, so she may not respond to even simple requests. When your dog is stressed, there are chemical changes going on in her body that prevent her from thinking clearly. This often leads to dogs reacting quickly and instinctively, which is not usually how we expect our dogs to act. If too many elements of stress are present at the same time and the dog feels like she cannot cope, she may act to defend herself, maybe even by biting.

Stress can begin to build in your dog's day to day activities. Stress tends to build on itself and accumulate over time. If your dog's stress level is already high, it won't take much to tip the scale and create a bad situation. Your dog may be able to handle a young child coming up to pet her on a normal day. But what if you are remodeling your house and your dog has to deal with strangers coming and going all day long for weeks on end, plus the noise (or vibrations) and commotion of power tools, people yelling to each other, a stressed out owner, etc? If you add a child trying to pet your dog into that mix, your dog may feel so overwhelmed by everything else going on that she snaps at the child, or worse.

So it's important to try to keep your dog's stress levels low in her daily life so she is better able to handle the unusual things that come her way. Be aware of when things are getting over the top. When will your dog's scale finally tip? Don't let it get to that point. Give your dog a time-out when needed. Protect her from getting overwhelmed. Use some stress-reducing techniques in your dog's daily life. And remember that your dog will react to your stress levels as well. Taking good care of yourself and keeping your own stress levels under control are good wellness care, but will also help you be that much closer to keeping your dog's stress levels under control.

Stress is not something to be scared of. It is normal and healthy for the body to react differently to certain things changing in the environment. It is what keeps us safe and allows us to avoid unpleasant and potentially dangerous situations. By keeping everyday stress levels low, you will allow your dog's body to be able to handle slightly stressful situations easily and return to a state of calm afterwards. By learning about your dog's stress signs, you will be able to help her to reduce her stress reactions while in the moment.

Tips for canine stress reduction

This is a collection of techniques and products that have worked for me in reducing a dog's stress levels and keeping them at low levels. It is important when dealing with ongoing stress behaviors that a thorough veterinary exam be completed as soon as possible. Many stress behaviors can be indicative of health concerns. These suggestions are in no way meant to replace veterinary care. Please take this list with you to your dog's veterinary appointment and ask which techniques and products would be suitable to try with your dog if you have any questions or concerns.

If your dog is in a situation she finds stressful, the easiest way to reduce her stress is to remove her from the area to a place that is calmer and quieter. If this is not possible, it may help for you to put an object or even your own body between your dog and what is causing her stress as a visual blocker (if your dog is able to see). Perhaps you can move her to a different vantage point which will help her to feel safer. For instance, moving her away from a busy doorway where others are coming and going will allow her to have more personal space.

If you have a crate with you that your dog recognizes as a safe place, use it. Place it in a quiet out-of-the-way place for your dog to relax in. Some dogs may find having the crate covered offers them a greater sense of security. If you don't have a crate with you, a few minutes in the safety of your car (a familiar environment to your dog) may help her to calm down.

Some dogs will appreciate a chew toy when they are stressed to help them self-soothe. Stuffed Kong toys and safe bones are good for this. Some dogs won't eat or chew when they are stressed, but others chew more when they are stressed. This will depend on your dog.

Gentle massage, TTouch®, Healing Touch for Animals®, and other body work can be helpful in teaching your dog to relax in stressful situations. Healing Touch for Animals® has a wonderful program where you can learn techniques for relaxing and calming your dog and for helping her to deal with stress, as does TTouch®.

Work slowly to get your dog used to new situations that may cause stress. Don't just throw her into a new situation and hope for the best. Your goal should always be to help your dog have an enjoyable experience. Go slowly so if she is not enjoying herself, you can intervene and remove her from the situation or make it easier for her.

Do not force your dog to interact with people or situations that are causing her stress. Let her approach as she becomes more comfortable.

There are supplements that can help with calming and relaxing your dog. Rescue remedy can be very useful to have on hand for stressful situations. Talk to your veterinarian about how best to use this supplement. Essential oils and other supplements can also be helpful, but care should be taken with dosages, so check with someone who is qualified to advise you.

Keeping a loose leash is a huge stress reducer! Dogs pulled around on tight leashes feel powerless and trapped and become fearful. Your dog can't relax if she feels that she cannot get away. Allow her to move away from the stress if she wishes. Teach loose leash walking.

Some dogs feel more comfortable when wearing a coat or T shirt. Check out other similar techniques and products such as TTouch®

body wraps, anxiety wraps, or Thundershirts. These create steady pressure to your dog's body and can be very calming.

Make sure your dog is getting enough exercise. Walking exercise is great! Allow your dog to sniff, using a long leash in an open area if you can. Dogs need to sniff and explore to feel secure in their environment. Walking gets your dog away from home and lets her experience new things and meet new people so she is better able to deal with the stresses of being in public. If she never leaves home, she can't be expected to know how to handle things outside of her home.

Change the dog's food to a more appropriate diet. Many popular dog foods have fillers and artificial ingredients that can affect your dog's behavior and body physiology, including how she deals with stress. A diet with better quality ingredients can help your dog feel better and be less stressed in general.

Let your dog have time to be a dog. Be less controlling when the situation does not call for it. Having the freedom to make some of her own decisions can boost her confidence and lower her stress levels.

Use calming music for your dog to listen to while you are away, or even while you are at home. Healing Touch for Animals® has great CDs created for this purpose, as does Through a Dog's Ear. Classical music can also work in a pinch. Of course this is only useful if your dog can hear the music. I have noticed that my b/d dog does appear to feel the vibrations of music through a radio on the floor.

Give your dog a safe place where she can choose to go get away from the world for a while. This may be a crate left open for her to come and go as she pleases, or a bed in a quiet corner where she won't be disturbed.

DAP sprays, collars, and plug-ins may be helpful in a variety of circumstances. DAP stands for dog-appeasing pheromones. DAP products were created to help soothe dogs in various situations.

Fears

In my experience, dogs with partial sight and/or partial hearing may show more fear reactions than dogs that cannot see or hear at all. Many dogs with partial hearing may hear and startle to a loud noise, but not be able to locate where the sound came from. It doesn't appear to be the sound itself that they are afraid of, but more the fact that they can't locate the source of the sound. Dogs that can hear normally will often startle to a loud noise, but then they go looking for the source of the sound and once they find it, they seem to be satisfied. Imagine yourself hearing loud booming noises from another room and not being able to find what was causing the noise. You would most likely be on edge until you found the cause of the noise. A dog that cannot locate the source of a startling noise will be on edge as well.

A dog with partial vision may also show more fear reactions. We cannot be fully certain what exactly it is that the dog sees, but she becomes familiar with her world the way she sees it. When anything in that world changes, it changes the entire picture of what she normally sees. With my own partially blind dog, she shows fear of anything new that appears in her known home environment … a new dog bed in the middle of the floor, a new person or a known person standing in a new place where she hasn't seen one before, a leaf bag in the back yard, etc. She is normally very confident and outgoing, but until she takes her time to explore whatever it is that looks different to her, she acts fearful of it. Sometimes it takes her a long time to approach and explore. Most times, she can judge by the other dogs' reactions that it's ok and she will approach much faster.

Some dogs may find it helpful if you put yourself near the new item and pat it and show the dog that everything is safe. Sometimes just sitting yourself near the thing that is scaring your dog will encourage her to settle down and approach. You should act as if nothing is out of the ordinary. If you act worried or stressed, your dog is likely to also feel worried or stressed.

Other dogs do better if just ignored and allowed to approach the item on their own and in their own time. If your dog really likes to eat, sprinkling very special treats around the area may help her to go exploring closer to the new person or object. But don't force her.

Scatter the food and then ignore her and let her choose when she is ready to approach.

Re-approaching the situation slowly and gradually may help most b/d dogs feel more confident to begin exploring the second time. Offering your lap or arms to sit in for security will not make the fear worse. It will give her some time to settle down and to get used to the situation while knowing she is safe. She will decide on her own when to explore. That's how she will gain confidence. It's normal for us to try to show the dog that everything is ok, but until she decides on her own that it is ok, she will continue to be wary of it.

Communicating with Your Blind/Deaf Dog

It's always a big concern to people; how do I possibly communicate with my blind and deaf dog? No, I cannot use gestures or words, but there are other ways to communicate. I can communicate with touch. Touch can involve anything the dog can feel through contact with its body. This can include intentional touch from my hands, as in touch cues for behaviors or information. It can include petting or massage type touching to help calm her, or just to let her know that I love her. It can mean more active petting or play type touching. It can involve the way the air currents and vibrations feel as I move past her or call her to me. She knows when I am just rolling over in bed at night, as opposed to when I sit up and am getting ready to get out of bed. She knows the differences between the vibrations of my footsteps vs. my son's steps.

We produce vibrations when we talk. Holding your b/d dog while you talk or sing to her is a soothing vibration as she rests against your chest or under your chin against your neck. She can feel the vibrations coming from you. The words we choose carry a certain vibration and energy all their own. I personally talk to my deaf dogs even though I know they can't hear me with their ears. But when we speak, our energy and emotion match what we are saying. For dogs that can see, our facial expressions and body posture match what we are saying. Words carry energy associated with what they mean to us. Telling your dog that you love her carries a whole different energy than telling her not to chew your best shoes! I have no doubt that dogs who are so in tune with the vibrations around them can also feel the difference in our words. So choose your words carefully, and then talk to your dog!

Have you ever walked into a room and felt that another person was in a bad mood? Nothing has to be said or done for you to feel the change in the air and know that something is not quite right. Our dogs can also feel our emotions. They can feel our state of mind through our touch – are you just touching her as you go through your day without really thinking about it? Are you touching her gently with love? Are you touching her playfully, to discipline her, or are you frustrated? Your dog can sense each of these. She will also sense your thoughts and emotions just from being close to you. It is important to keep your thoughts clear and positive. Try to send your dog a clear picture with your mind about what you want her to do. You may be surprised at how quickly your dog will catch on the next time you are trying to teach her something new!

Just a note about touch cues – I have found through trial and error that I can communicate more clearly with Treasure by touching her lightly first to get her attention before giving her a cue or sign. This prevents her from startling as she would if I just gave her a touch sign out of the blue, which would probably cause her to miss what I was trying to tell her. By touching her first, she has a moment to realize that I'm there and want her attention. Then I can tell her what I want to convey and she is ready to respond.

Naming and explaining

Adding cues to every day happenings

"Once I knew only darkness and stillness ... my life was without past or future ... but a little word from the fingers of another fell into my hand that clutched at emptiness and my heart leaped to the rapture of living." ~Helen Keller

When I read the above quote, I can only begin to imagine the excitement that Helen Keller felt as she realized the meaning of her first words. For so long, she had lived in silence and darkness at the whim of others, with little understanding of the world around her. I imagine our b/d dogs feel something similar. Do they know why we lead or carry them here and there? Do they have any idea where they are going or why?

When I first adopted Treasure, it seemed odd to live next to this being that only lived in silence and darkness. She accepted my handling and learned the routine as well as her way around the house and yard. But I wanted to find a way to tell her about her day. I wanted to open up her world to the excitement of anticipating a walk or a ride in the car. I started to teach her touch cues for different activities in her day.

Dogs that are able to see notice things in their environments that give them a clue about what is about to happen. We may pick up a leash or a food bowl or walk towards the door to let them out. Dogs that can hear may notice the jingle of our keys when a car ride is imminent. We also tend to talk to our dogs, which also clues them in to what is going to happen next.

I think it adds a dimension of enjoyment to our dogs' lives to give them something to look forward to, to create some anticipation in their lives. Think of how excited a dog gets when it's mealtime or time for a walk. Why should our b/d dogs be any different? They just need to gather information in different ways. By teaching our dogs touch cues for the things they do every day; we can add that dimension of excitement into their lives as well.

Think of things and activities that are important to you and your dog throughout a typical day. You might want to write down a list. Most likely, your dog will need to go outside several times a day to do her business and for play and exercise. All dogs like to eat, so your dog will have one or more mealtimes each day. There may be car rides, walks, play time, cuddle on the couch time, bedtime - the possibilities are endless.

Don't try to teach everything all at once. This is a new process for both of you. You will need to learn and remember each new sign and incorporate it into your handling of your dog consistently. Your dog will need to learn the new signs. She may not have had someone try to communicate with her before, so this whole process may be new to her. Once she catches on to the fact that you are trying to communicate with her, future signs will probably be learned much faster than in the beginning.

Choose the activity on your list that happens most often (I will choose going outside for my example). Immediately before this activity happens, give your dog the touch cue you have decided upon for that activity. The closer the new cue can be to the activity, the quicker your dog will learn to associate the two together.

Begin with your dog at the door with you. Immediately before you open the door to let her outside, give her the touch cue for outside. Then quickly open the door and take your dog outside. Every time you take your dog outside, use the outside touch cue and soon you will begin to see your dog anticipate what will happen next. Maybe you will see a wag of the tail, or a lift of the head, but you will begin to see some signal of understanding from your dog that she knows what is coming next and is eager to go outside.

If your dog knows her way to the door, you can then start to give the touch cue a very short distance from the door. Then quickly help your dog to the door and outside. Gradually, you can move back farther from the door and when you give the outside cue, your dog will learn to go to the door and wait for you to let her outside.

Follow the same idea for teaching other activity cues. Add the new cue immediately before the activity. Always use the same cue to mean the same thing. If you mix up the cues, your dog will be confused. For this reason, I only teach a couple new cues at a time, so I can keep track of them all in my head! It's also helpful to write them down on your list.

If you have other family members, it's important that each person gives the same cues to the dog. Posting your list where it's easy to refer to can be helpful in the beginning to keep everyone on the same page. Don't give a cue unless you are in a position to then make sure the activity happens. If you give your dog cues for things that don't happen, she will start to ignore the cues because they won't mean anything to her.

Some ideas for naming and explaining cues

These are the ones we use most frequently. I'm sure you will think of many of your own.

Outside: I use the sign language cue for out while touching the side of Treasure's face. I begin with a teardrop-shaped hand (all fingers touching tip of thumb), place the back of my fingers against her cheek and draw my hand up, forward, and away from her face, ending in the air near her nose.

Inside, going back to the house: I use the sign language cue for home. Begin with a teardrop-shaped hand. Touch tips of all fingers and thumb to side of dog's nose and then again quickly to side of her ear. Hand should be removed from her face in between, not slid against the side of the face.

Car ride: Begin with a closed fist. Place the fist, thumb side down, on dog's shoulder. Move hand, while maintaining contact with dog, up over the dog's back and to her other shoulder, and then move hand back to original shoulder. Imagine running your hand over the top arc of a steering wheel.

Mealtime: Begin by using a tear-shaped hand, as if you are holding something small between all your fingers and your thumb. Then tap all fingertips and thumb against her chin. For a small dog, you can just use a finger to tap her chin.

More about cues

Cues can be given in many forms. A cue is just a signal to the dog that something is going to happen, or that they have the opportunity to earn reinforcement by doing something that we've taught them.

Visual cues: If your dog has some vision, you may be able to use hand signals close to her face as cues. Your ability to use hand signals may change depending upon how light or dark the environment is, or on how far away you are from your dog. Wearing white gloves may help your hands and signals to be more obvious to your dog. If your dog can recognize the difference between light and dark, you may be able to use light cues to communicate certain things to your dog. For instance, flashing the porch light at night may be enough to let your b/d dog know that it's time to come back inside from the yard. Turning off the bedroom light at night may be enough to let her know that it's bedtime.

Audible cues: If your dog can hear, you may be able to use spoken or other noise cues. Maybe your dog can hear some loud noises, but can't differentiate between spoken words. A loud whistle or other noise can become a signal for your dog to come to you. Your dog may be able to hear a loud clicker or other marker signal to assist with teaching her new things.

Texture cues: Textures are part of our everyday life. You can create cues for your b/d dog using various textures and the changes from one texture to another. You can use textures to help your dog create a map around your house and yard. She will learn to judge where she is by what textures are around her. For instance, throw rugs in the kitchen or by the back door, dog beds, carpet vs. tile or hardwood, grass vs. gravel or mulch in the yard, etc. It is best not to move these textures around unnecessarily, because your dog will become confused if she is expecting to find a landmark and it is suddenly not there, or she finds it in a different area. She will eventually adjust to new locations, but it is kindest to not move them unless it's absolutely necessary.

Some of the ways you can use textures as landmarks for your dog are:

Place carpet mats by doors in your home that she will use frequently. You can also use outdoor carpet mats to show her where the door is to come back inside. A mat under the food and water bowls will allow your dog to feel with her feet when she is getting close and slow down before stepping in or spilling the bowls. Mats may also be helpful to signal the top and bottom of flights of stairs. Carpet runners can define hallways or other areas of your home. Make sure all mats and throw rugs have a non-slip backing to keep them in place. Bathroom rugs work great for this too!

You can define certain areas of the yard by putting mulch around trees and other barriers. Your dog will learn to slow down when her feet touch the mulch so she can avoid running into the trees. I use a small border fence line to define areas where I don't want Treasure to go. She is a small dog, so this usually works to keep her out, but she also uses the small fence line to find her way around the yard, especially when it snows and she can't feel the same textures on the ground that she's used to.

Brick or stone walkways outside are enjoyable for us to look at, yet can also be used by your dog to find her way around. She will soon learn where the path leads and you will see her beginning to feel with her feet for where the path begins and ends.

You can also use textures as cues for different behaviors. You can teach your dog to wait out of the kitchen while you are cooking. Because she can't see or hear you, it can be dangerous to have her underfoot sniffing out food while you are trying to carry pots of hot water to the sink. If your kitchen has a boundary line where carpet meets tile, you can use that texture boundary to teach her where to wait.

You can create a stay mat. Teach your dog to stay on a particular mat. Choose a mat with a texture that will stand out to her. Once you teach this, you can take the mat with you anywhere to be able to leave your dog waiting patiently on the mat while you do other things. This can be very handy when traveling. That stay mat can then be used to define a place for her to ride in the car, transfer her to a new crate, when camping in a tent, to get her to stay in a stroller or wagon on walks – you get the idea.

You will only be limited by your own creativity! Mats can be found in many different textures: carpet (different lengths of pile create different textures), straw, rubber, wooden, plastic, vinyl, stone or pebble, cork, etc. If you want a challenge, teach your dog that each texture is a cue for a different behavior to be done on that particular mat. Don't limit your dog. Have fun challenging her. See how much you can teach her.

Scent cues: Our dog's world is a smorgasbord of scents! Her sense of smell is so much more sophisticated than ours. She can smell so many things that we can't. Treasure can tell the difference in scent between the toenail clippers and her brush when it's grooming time. She can smell her eye drops, even though I can find no discernible odor. Don't underestimate how well your b/d dog can smell. She may surprise you!

Some people recommend scenting different rooms or areas of the house with different odors to help your b/d dog. Personally, I know I am not organized enough to keep each individual scent refreshed, always use the same exact brands of scent, and remember which room has which scent. But I also know that dogs have magnificent noses and can already tell the difference in scents around the house. Even in a new house, the first thing they do is go sniff out every nook and cranny. The bedroom smells different from the kitchen, the living room, and the bathroom. I have not had any problem with any of my b/d dogs learning their way around without adding extra odors. That being said, I try to minimize using cleaning agents that have a strong smell, or I let them air out after cleaning, when the dogs are aren't around. Harsh-smelling cleaners can mask the regular room odors.

Give your b/d dog some time to get to know the new house. If you find that after a couple weeks, your dog is still having trouble finding her way around, you can try putting a scent on only a few places where you want your dog to go. For instance, the door to go outside is probably an important one. You can put some scent on the mat by the door, or you can hang a scent on the doorknob. Try to use a scent that you don't use in other places in your home. If you use vanilla extract to scent the door, but then you use vanilla in the kitchen while cooking a lot, you can see where there might be some confusion, and the scent at the door won't stand out as much for your dog.

Remember when using scents that your dog's nose is so much more sensitive than yours. She can smell things that you can't. If you use scents that are too strong, you may actually end up repelling your dog away from the area, rather than attracting her to it. When using scent with your dog, less is more.

There are scented dog toys which may interest your dog. Tennis balls come with different scents or you can make your own by putting tennis balls in a sealed bag with a small amount of odor. The tennis balls will absorb some of the odor. Other hard plastic or rubber toys sometimes come with a sweet vanilla odor.

I use scent as cues for everyday activities. The smell of the eye drops means I will soon expect her to cooperate while I put drops in her eyes, but then she will get a cuddle and extra treats. The smell of the dog brush means I will groom her now. The smell of nail clippers means that I will be laying her on her back and cutting her nails. The smell of her leash means I am about to clip it to her collar and then we are going out for an adventure. I don't add any special scent to these items. They each carry their own individual scent which my dogs can tell apart from the others. I can tell because their reactions to each item are different.

Tactile cues: Tactile cues include all cues given when you touch your dog, but they also include cues that your dog feels from the environment around her. This can include texture cues, but in this category I'm referring more to vibrations and air currents that signal certain things to your dog. Tactile cues also include cues that you give your dog through the use of equipment like collars, harnesses and leashes.

I will discuss later in the book how to teach new behaviors to your b/d dog and how to add touch cues to those behaviors. It is important to remember to be consistent with the touch cues that you choose. In the beginning it is easiest to choose places to touch on your dog's body that are not too close together to keep each cue very clear and separate from the others. As your dog learns more and more touch cues, you may be able to introduce touches that are closer to each other on her body, but that may be too confusing to her in the beginning. Be sure to touch your dog neutrally first to get her attention before giving a specific cue for a behavior. This gives her a moment to turn her attention to you so she will be able to recognize the cue.

You can use touch cues for things besides specific behaviors as well. Your b/d dog may enjoy being held or rocked gently. She may be soothed by feeling the vibrations of you humming or singing while holding her against your chest.

Your dog will learn what different vibrations and air currents in her environment mean. She will use this information to sense what is going on around her and what is going to happen next based on her daily routine. You can also use vibrations to help you better communicate with your dog. Wooden decks and ramps carry vibrations very well. A stomp on the wooden ramp outside lets Treasure know I am at the door and it is time to come up the ramp and into the house. She can also tell as I walk down the ramp to the yard which direction I am going and she joins me down in the grass. As long as you are consistent in the vibration cues you give, your dog will figure it out.

You can tap the floor with your foot or walk a bit heavier to let your dog know you are approaching or that you are leaving the room. Don't sneak up next to your dog and stomp hard. This will startle her. Just use enough vibration through the floor to get her attention. I have found that some floors carry vibrations in the direction that I am moving and some do not. In my kitchen, Treasure can follow the vibrations of my footsteps in the direction that I am walking. A concrete floor with rubber mats does not produce much of a vibration. And on some floors, she can feel the vibrations, but she doesn't know which way to look, because the vibrations don't travel with my direction. Then I need to step in with different cues to let her know which direction I'm headed. If I want Treasure to know I am moving in a different direction, I may brush my leg gently past her in that direction so she can feel the movement.

How Dogs Learn

When your dog does a behavior, there are consequences that happen afterwards. Some of those consequences are things that your dog likes, and some are things that she doesn't like. If something happens that she likes, she will tend to do that behavior more and more because her behavior was reinforced. When something happens that she doesn't like, she will tend to avoid doing that behavior again. Dogs learn on their own from consequences all the time. And, yes, b/d dogs learn in the same way!

Reinforced behavior tends to get repeated. What each dog finds reinforcing may differ from the preferences of other dogs. And what your particular dog finds reinforcing may not be what you expected. In order for your dog to want to repeat the behavior, she must think the consequence is reinforcing. If the consequence is not something she cares about, she won't find it exciting enough to repeat the behavior.

You will need to take some time to find out what your dog thinks is reinforcing (rewarding). Some dogs like physical petting, but some don't. Some like to play special games or play with special toys. Many like food treats, but some may need higher value treats than others to motivate them. You must learn to take control of the most special things in your dog's life and use those things to reinforce behaviors that you like. You don't need to limit the things she likes, but you should be mindful that you are not offering those resources at the wrong times. Unwanted behaviors can also be reinforced and will happen more and more if you are not careful.

So, for example, most dogs like to go outside. If your dog is sitting nicely at the door (the behavior) and you then open the door so she can go out (the consequence that she likes), you have just reinforced the behavior of sitting nicely at the door. If you continue to open the door only when your dog is sitting nicely, you will soon start to notice that she is sitting more and more, waiting for you to open the door. If your dog is jumping up and barking in her excitement to go outside (the behavior) and you then open the door quickly to let her go out (the consequence she likes), you have just reinforced the behavior of jumping up and barking, and this behavior will tend to happen more and more when she wants to go outside. So the same consequence can reinforce two very different behaviors. It is up to you which one you want to encourage.

Sometimes unwanted behavior continues to happen even if you aren't reinforcing it. If the behavior is continuing, something must be happening that your dog finds rewarding. If your dog continues to run back and forth barking with the neighbor's dog on the other side of the fence, then she is finding that activity reinforcing on some level. If your dog is continuing to raid the trash can day after day, then she is finding something yummy inside that she finds reinforcing.

If you find yourself wondering why some of these unwanted behaviors are happening, look at the situation from your dog's perspective. What is she getting out of the deal that she finds rewarding? If you can change the consequence so that it's not rewarding to her, you are on your way to changing her behavior. Once the consequence is changed, you must also create an alternative behavior that you do like and make that behavior more rewarding than the previous behavior. With consistency, your dog will decide she would rather do the new behavior and get the reward, than do the previous behavior and get a consequence that she doesn't like as much.

Your dog will learn fastest through patient repetition and consistency. If you get frustrated, your dog will become confused. She won't understand why you are treating her differently or why you are upset. Every time you see behavior that you like, reward it quickly. The reward must come immediately after or during the behavior. If you wait too long, the reward will still be nice for the dog, but it won't be as clear to her what you are rewarding.

Things dogs like

This is a short list of things that dogs may find reinforcing to get you started thinking and making your own list. Of course, the items that can be added to this list are endless. Create a list of things that your dog finds reinforcing so you can use those things to teach her behaviors you like.

What dogs like - trash cans, new smells, rolling in smelly or dirty stuff, digging holes, chasing squirrels, playing with other dogs, swimming, attention, freedom, squeaky toys, tennis balls, riding in the car, going for a walk, going in or out doors, food!, belly rubs, coming out of a kennel or crate, children, chasing bicycles, hotdogs, chewing, barking, going to the bathroom, eating grass, hunting, following smells, going fast, going to new places, petting, ear scratches, butt scratches, mealtime, frisbee, the park, cats, de-stuffing dog toys, and so on ...

Tips to make training successful

Catch your dog doing something right! Always be prepared to reinforce behaviors you like. Try to reward while your dog is still doing what you like!

Dogs do what works! If a dog's actions get her something that she enjoys, she will continue to do those behaviors. If a dog's actions cause something she doesn't like, she will stop doing those behaviors. It is really that simple.

Reduce stress! Dogs and humans do not learn well when they are stressed. If you or your dog are stressed, stop training and try again later. Reducing stress in your dog's daily life will help her to be more receptive when it is time to learn new things.

Plan ahead and set your dog up to be successful. Set up the environment so your dog will make good behavior choices. For example, do not leave the chicken on the table while you leave the room, unless you take the dog with you! Or, unless you want the dog to eat the chicken!

Dogs react to our thoughts and emotions. Think positively! Instead of thinking about what you don't want your dog to do, create a lovely picture in your mind of what you DO want her to do instead. Then help to make it happen.

What you use to reward your dog must be something your dog thinks is special! I know I've already said that, but it's important to remember. It isn't enough for you to think it's special. Use whatever it is that gets your dog excited, even if it's not your choice at the time. You will get better effort out of your dog.

Reinforcing behavior you like

One of the first things to teach your b/d dog is a signal that means good job – I like that you did that. You will use this signal to teach your dog new things and to reinforce behaviors that you like so they will happen more often in the future. The signal can be anything you wish as long as it can be given quickly and consistently.

If your dog has any vision at all, you may be able to use a thumbs-up hand signal near her face as a good dog signal. Deaf dogs also take cues from your body language and expressions, so when you give the thumbs up signal, make sure your body and face look happy. I usually talk to my deaf dogs when I sign good dog. My face is happy as I am speaking and my body motions convey my excitement. Our bodies take on the energy of our words and our posture and movements are affected by the words we say.

For your b/d dog, use touch to show her she did something you liked. Your dog probably has favorite places to be scratched. You should still talk to her when you pet her. Remember that your body responds differently dependent upon your words and the intention behind those words. Your touch will feel different if you are happy, frustrated, tired, or excited. You will be able to calm your dog with your touch, and you will be able to excite and energize her with your touch as well. Talking to her at the same time is natural for you, and will help her to feel the correct intention.

You will probably need to teach your new dog what the good dog signal means. Find several things that your dog already likes. For many dogs these include food treats, toys, petting, going in or out of a door, etc. You should already have a list of some things that your dog likes. Give the good dog signal and then immediately give her something that she likes. If you choose petting as your good dog signal, it may already be rewarding to your dog by itself. But be aware that some dogs just don't like petting all that much. You can teach her to think of petting as a good thing by following it up with something she really likes a lot. But if your dog just doesn't seem to like petting, use something else as your good dog signal.

Follow up the good dog signal with things your dog likes until she starts to respond to the good dog signal by anticipating the treat or other special thing. You will need to do this many times. After she understands that the good dog signal is a good thing, begin to use it at other times during the day. Use it when your dog does something you like and then follow up with a treat or special thing. In the beginning it's a good idea to continue to use the treat (special thing) after the good dog signal to really cement its importance into your dog's mind.

As time goes on, you can use the good dog signal with other rewards – life rewards. If your dog normally jumps and barks at the back door to go outside, you can reward that short moment of calm and quiet by signaling good dog and then letting your dog outside quickly. If your dog gives you the toy nicely at playtime, use the good dog signal and then play with the toy again as the reward.

Try to always associate the good dog signal with things that your dog likes. You won't always have to follow it with another reward, but do be aware of how you are using it and every now and then follow it up with a very special reward.

Clickers and other marker signals

Sometimes in training, you may want a very quick and specific way to pinpoint small parts of behaviors. If you teach your dog a marker signal, you can use it like a camera to point out a very small part of the behavior that you really liked, so it will be repeated again. There are many books and resources out there about clicker training, so I will not get into the specifics here. The clicker is a tool and is not necessary for training your dog, but it is a good tool to have if you are really into teaching your dog new things! I do a lot of marker (clicker) training. It's a lot of fun. Check into it if you're interested.

What I will discuss here, however, is how to adapt the clicker for your blind/deaf dog if you choose to use one. Once you've chosen which marker signal to use, you teach it the same way as a clicker, and you use it the same way as the clicker.

If your dog can hear a clicker, you may choose to use one for your marker signal. If your dog cannot hear a clicker or a verbal marker signal, you will need to think about other alternatives. If your dog has any vision, a penlight flash may work as a marker signal. In a bright room or outside, however, the penlight can be hard for the dog to notice unless they are looking directly at the penlight. A dog with vision may be able to see a hand signal, but it must be something that you can do very fast. A fist flashed open into an open hand and quickly back into a fist may work. You will need to practice whichever marker signal you choose to improve your timing if you decide to do this kind of training.

With my deaf dogs, I use a flashed thumbs-up signal for my marker. With my b/d dog, I use a tactile marker signal. I use a double tap quickly on her shoulder. You can choose any tactile signal that works for you and your dog, just keep it consistent.

Once you have chosen which marker signal to use, you need to teach your dog what it means. Give the marker signal one time and immediately follow it with a special treat. Repeat this process over and over again until your dog starts to respond to the marker by anticipating the reward that comes afterward. This shouldn't take very long, but do a couple short sessions this way before you actually start training. It is important with marker training that the marker signal always be followed up with the treat reward. The marker is a promise to your dog that a treat is coming soon! Don't break that promise.

Practicing your timing will allow you to have the most success with marker training. If your timing is not good, you may end up trying to mark one behavior, but really marking something you didn't intend to reinforce. Read about clicker training so you understand the principles involved. Then you can begin using the marker signal during training sessions.

Interrupting behaviors you don't like

It's all well and good to talk about praising and rewarding your dog for behavior you like. But what about when she does things that you don't like? Corrections may sometimes stop the behavior temporarily, but they really don't teach your dog how you do want her to behave instead. This creates stress.

When your dog does something you don't like, interrupt her so the behavior stops. You can interrupt behaviors by doing something to get her attention. A surprise stomp on the floor might work, a surprise touch on the hip, using a spray bottle of water to hit her on the hip, etc. A spray bottle or a stomp can be used if you are too far away from your dog to touch her immediately, but you should be on your way over to your dog when you use them. I use a spray or a stomp if I see my dog doing something that needs to stop immediately and may be dangerous. Otherwise, I go to my dog and touch her to distract her from whatever she is doing.

You should always use the least amount of intervention needed to get your dog's attention, so if a gentle touch is enough to get her attention, then that is all you should use. As your dog becomes more tuned in to you, she may require less intervention than she might need in the beginning.

The interruption process continues after you distract her from the behavior. You then need to quickly redirect her behavior to something more appropriate. In the beginning, this may mean gently removing her from the area to a more appropriate one, handing her something more appropriate to chew, etc. As you teach her more signs and behaviors, you will have more options for redirecting and telling her what you prefer she do instead.

After you have redirected your dog to do something more appropriate, it is important to praise and reinforce your dog so she learns that the new behavior is more reinforcing than the previous one. So the entire process of interrupting behavior you don't like is: interrupt the unwanted behavior, redirect your dog to do something more appropriate, and then praise and reinforce the new behavior.

Adding cues to new behaviors

There are different ways to add a new cue to a behavior. First, you must realize that the cue does not make the behavior happen. The dog chooses whether to do the behavior or not. The cue is a signal to your dog that you are asking her to do a particular behavior now, and that if she does it correctly; she has a chance to earn reinforcement (something she likes). Your dog doesn't start out knowing what the cue means. Each cue needs to be taught to her.

I teach some cues by repeating the cue as I'm helping the dog do the behavior. Over time, the dog will come to associate the two together. Because of the logistics of using our hands to help a b/d dog into the behaviors, it is often easier to also have the way we touch them become the cue. If you are teaching a dog to sit that will not follow a food lure and you are helping her to sit by using your hands, the placement of your hands will become associated with the behavior in your dog's mind. It is easiest to then fade that touch slightly until it becomes the touch cue for the sit behavior.

For other cues, I will teach the behavior first, until the dog is doing it quickly and easily with very little assistance on my part to get her started. At that point, I can decide on what I want the cue to be and insert the cue immediately before the dog does the behavior. If I am teaching my dog to sit using a food lure and I know that every time I move the food lure upward near her nose, she sits, I am then ready to add the cue. I give the touch cue for sit, then immediately lure my dog into the sit position, and then reinforce her.

By adding the new cue immediately before the behavior, she learns that the cue is an indicator that a particular behavior (in this case sit) will be reinforced. After many repetitions, I can then give the cue and wait with a slight pause before luring her to see if she will sit on her own, and then I can reward her.

This is the process used to teach new cues for behaviors. It doesn't matter which type of cue you choose to use – visual, spoken, tactile, etc. They are all learned the same way.

Manners and Everyday Life

It's always easier to prevent unwanted behavior before it becomes a habit than to try to stop that behavior later. With a puppy or new dog, it's important to manage her environment until she knows the rules of the house. Use gates to keep her in the rooms where you are, so you can watch what she's doing. Remember to reward behaviors that you like so they will continue. Interrupt behaviors that you don't like and then redirect her to other more suitable behaviors so you can reward those.

Here are some common behaviors and issues that you may need to deal with as your dog is acclimating to your home and routine.

Bite inhibition

All dogs have teeth. All dogs have the ability to bite. Many dogs will never bite a person during their lifetimes. Other dogs may bite only when they are scared or in pain. Dogs that have been taught to be gentle with their mouths will cause less damage if they should ever bite. Many people think that deaf dogs are more likely to bite than other dogs. This is not true. Again, all dogs have the ability to bite, deaf or not. It is important that we teach all dogs to use their mouths gently and to be respectful of human skin.

Teaching your b/d dog to control the strength of her mouth is very important. This is a critical skill for any dog to learn, but sometimes dogs that can't hear have trouble learning it. These lessons begin when the dog is still a puppy with its mother and littermates. When one puppy bites another too hard, the one that is being bitten will yelp sharply. This often startles the first puppy into letting go. The puppy learns that in order to continue playing with the other puppies, it needs to control the strength of its mouth. Since puppies play with their mouths, they learn to grip each other with less and less pressure. It's important that puppies learn this skill while their teeth are small and not as likely to cause major damage. As they get older, their adult teeth will appear and will cause much more damage if they haven't learned to be gentle.

When a puppy enters a human household, it needs to also learn to control its mouth with its new human family. Human skin is even more fragile than dog skin, so the puppy needs to learn to be even more careful with us than with other dogs. Our natural reaction when something hurts is to blurt out "ouch!" This will often stop a puppy that can hear. Some puppies are more persistent than others and continue to bite too hard, but most will be startled and will stop and look at you.

Obviously, b/d puppies cannot hear the yelp or our "ouch," and may have trouble learning to be gentle. This is not an excuse since this is such an important skill for dogs to learn. B/d puppies must still be taught how to be gentle. Here are some ideas that I have found helpful.

Some puppies will learn to be gentle if you give them a time out every time they bite too hard. When your dog bites too hard (usually during playtime), give her a stop that signal. I use a tiny (gentle) tap twice on the top of the dog's muzzle while I say "stop that." This is not a correction and is not hitting the puppy. It's just a light touch. Then, immediately remove yourself from her reach. Move your body part away quickly and stand up so she can't reach you. If you repeatedly try to push your puppy away, you may be making the situation worse. Puppies tend to see pushing and shoving as play behavior and may think you are enjoying the game. Instead, move away from your puppy's reach and just wait.

Once your dog calms down, even for a moment, give your good dog sign gently and then slowly and calmly return to her level. Begin to interact again, but calmly and gently. You must be consistent and end the interaction every time she bites too hard or plays too roughly.

If you always follow the stop that signal with a time out, you will begin to notice your puppy responding to the signal before you can give the time out. At that point, you can stop giving the time out. Just give your stop signal and when your puppy pauses and settles give your good dog signal and interact again calmly.

Handing your puppy a bone or toy to chew on can help to redirect the mouthing behaviors. Puppies do need to chew and they explore and learn about the world through their mouths. It is not realistic to expect a puppy to never use her mouth. It is your responsibility to teach your puppy how and when it is appropriate to use her mouth. Provide lots of toys and bones for the puppy to chew on.

If you have tried the time outs for a few weeks and the behavior is not getting any better, you can try using a spray bottle full of plain water. Set the water bottle's nozzle so the water comes out as a stream instead of a mist. The pressure of the stream will help to get your puppy's attention. It is important to try to keep the spray bottle concealed if you can. Otherwise, many puppies will learn to only control themselves if they see or smell the water bottle near you.

Keep the spray bottle near you, but tucked behind your back or on a table nearby where you can reach it easily. When your puppy bites down on you too roughly, give the stop that signal as you reach behind you to get the spray bottle. Immediately after the stop signal, spray the bottle one time, making sure that the stream hits the puppy. Aim for a place on the puppy's body, not its face. By aiming at the puppy's body, you increase the startle factor as it will probably turn to look at what just touched it. Put the spray bottle behind your back again. If the puppy has stopped and turned its attention elsewhere, give the good dog signal and resume a calm interaction.

By timing the spray to occur after the stop that signal (not at the same time as), you will eventually be able to stop using the water. Your puppy will begin to stop when you give the stop that signal in anticipation of the spray of water coming next. When you see this reaction, stop using the spray bottle. Be quick to give the good dog signal as soon as you see your puppy stop herself and then resume interacting gently.

It is important to end each session with calm and gentle interacting. Any time you interrupt a behavior you don't like, you need to then show your puppy the behavior that you do want instead. It is also important to end each session with something enjoyable for the puppy. End the session when she is interacting appropriately. It is tempting to keep going and going when things are going well. But puppies have short attention spans. A short period of time when things are going well can teach her a lot.

Chewing

Chewing is a natural dog behavior, but dogs often choose to chew things that we don't want them to chew! Dog-proofing your house and putting away your valuable things will help with this. Keeping your dog near you where you can see what she's doing, will allow you to intervene quickly if you see her choosing to chew something inappropriate. Make sure she has lots of appropriate toys and bones to chew on and substitute one of those when you need to redirect her.

When you see her chewing on something appropriate, sometimes walk past and drop a tasty treat near her to reward her for chewing the correct items. This will also begin to teach her that she doesn't need to protect her belongings. She will learn that you approaching when she has a toy leads to good things!

When you need to leave your dog alone, make sure she is in an area that is dog-proofed and leave her with many good choices about things she is allowed to chew. Some dogs chew when they are anxious, so if your dog gets anxious when she is left alone, she may chew even more when you're gone.

Resource guarding

It is natural for dogs to become protective of things they value. This is not usually a behavior that humans appreciate and it can be dangerous in human society. It is your job to teach your dog not to protect her belongings from you. This is easiest to teach with a puppy, but a new dog will also need to learn it. You must be more cautious with a dog that has already learned to protect her things. It may be necessary to work with a professional trainer in the beginning to keep everyone safe.

With a b/d dog, it's important to let your dog know that you are nearby before trying to touch her when she has something of value. Remember that it is the dog's perception of value that matters. A tissue she has stolen from the trashcan may be just as valuable to your dog as a roast stolen from the kitchen table or as her favorite stuffed toy. Some dogs also try to protect places of value – a favorite dog bed, a place on the couch, etc.

This is training that should always be done by an adult (not a child). As you pass your dog and she is busy chewing or playing with a toy, or she is snuggled on the dog bed or the end of the couch, sometimes drop tasty treats down right next to her. In the beginning, drop them so your hand can stay up and away from your dog in case she decides to snap. Your dog doesn't need to do anything to get the treat. You are associating your presence and your approach with good things. The idea is that your dog will begin to look forward to you approaching in case you have that special treat. With a b/d dog, you will need to drop the treats so they touch her slightly as they land. She will then turn to see what happened and will smell the treats there.

If this is going well after a couple weeks, you can progress to the next step. Be sure you are using very high value goodies. The value of the goodies you are using should be more than whatever your dog is already interacting with. As you approach, watch for signs that your dog knows you are approaching. The idea is not to surprise her. The idea is that she recognizes that you are there and will allow you to approach her. Tapping your foot on the floor near her or wiggling the dog bed a bit with your foot may let her know that you are there.

Drop a goodie right near her like before. As she eats, drop another one. As she finishes the second one, hopefully she is now looking for the next goodie and you can tempt her to come towards the treat in your hand. Do not reach for whatever the item is at this point. You are still conditioning her to think that you being there is a good thing. Feed her a treat or two from your hand and then move on with your day. It's good to leave her wanting more.

Do this in many different situations and places over the next few weeks. If you are ever concerned about your dog's reaction, seek professional help. Don't try to force the issue.

When this step is going well, you can begin to use those treats to lure your dog off the dog bed or couch. Approach her and make sure she knows you are there. By this time, she should be quickly orienting to you and wondering if you brought those great treats. Reward her for moving off and away from the area she was resting in and coming towards you. In the beginning, you may need to reward small movements in your direction, but as you progress, expect her to come all the way off the resting area to you to get her treats.

If she is chewing an object, you can begin to play trading games. Approach and be sure she knows you are there. Feed some treats from your hand. As she is eating, reach over with your other hand and touch the item she was chewing on and then remove your hand. Keep feeding treats. If things are going well, you can pick up the item on your next reach and then set it down again. Keep feeding a few more treats and then end the session.

You get the idea of how you can progress with this. Throughout your dog's lifetime you should play trading games, where you take things from your dog in exchange for something really special. When playing these games, always try to give the same item back to your dog at the end of the session. Dogs are more likely to be protective of items that they know they will not get back. If it's a safe and appropriate item for your dog to have, play some trading games for special goodies, and then hand the item back to your dog to end the session.

Sometimes your dog will have something that is dangerous for her or is of value to you. In these situations, you will be happy that you have played trading games! Don't panic. Remain calm and go get the special goodies quickly. Approach your dog and begin playing the trading games and feeding the great food liberally. Get the item from your dog. Continue feeding for a bit longer and then try to substitute a different item to give back to your dog.

Staying alone

Every dog will one day need to stay alone. Being alone is not natural for your dog. They enjoy being part of a group. You should teach your dog to be comfortable staying alone even if you don't think there will be much need for it. Hardly anyone stays home with their dog 24/7. There is grocery shopping to be done, friends to visit, etc. Even if you are home 24/7 with your dog, what happens if she gets sick and has to spend the night at the vet's office without you? Your dog will be much calmer if you have already taught her to tolerate being away from you.

Begin by leaving your dog behind a gate or in a pen or crate for short calm periods of time while you are still home. Your dog will know that you are nearby, but will get used to being separated from you a bit. Work on this at times when your dog is already calm. Trying to work on it at your dog's mealtime or when there is a lot of activity in the house is not when your dog is likely to be calm.

If your dog panics, comfort her but don't baby her. Don't ignore a dog that is panicking. Her fear will continue to escalate and you will undo any good training you've already done. Try to keep her behind the gate if you can and just go sit next to the opposite side of the gate so she can get close to you at first. You can reach through to touch her. When she settles, try to let her out of the area or go into the area with her while she is calm. Let her know that her being calm will bring you back to her.

As your dog is tolerating staying alone and is fairly calm, you can begin to step out for brief periods of time. With a b/d dog, you may be able to easily sneak out or you may not. The idea is not to sneak out and then stay gone for a long time. You must give your dog many short calm periods of time without you for her to become comfortable that you will return. Step out of the room to get something and then come back. As your dog is staying calm with this, you can begin to leave for longer periods of time. Vary the amount of time you're gone.

There are things that can help your dog stay alone more comfortably. You can keep her busy with enrichment items. Vary the items that you use so each day is different for her. Sometimes having her special bed or blanket with her will offer comfort, or something with your scent on it to snuggle with. Placing a radio on the floor outside the gate may offer some vibrations from soothing music. Your dog may appreciate this or not, so experiment. Keeping the radio on the floor will allow the vibrations to transfer into your dog's space while keeping the cords out of her reach on the other side of the gate.

Stress reduction tools may also help your dog to stay alone without being anxious. DAP sprays can be used on your dog's bed or blanket. DAP plug-ins or collars can be in place at all times.

Quiet

One of the first questions I am often asked about my deaf and b/d dogs is if they bark. Oh yes, and boy, can they bark! It is important to me that my dogs don't bark on and on and on, and I have breeds that are known to bark more than others. So I teach them to be quiet when told.

Begin by paying attention to your dog when she is quiet. Offer calm petting and praise and give your quiet cue intermittently while you are petting as long as she is being quiet. Name that state of her being quiet by giving the quiet signal at times when she is quiet, and pair it with calm praise and petting. You may even want to give a treat – just make sure the dog is quiet for the whole process.

When the dog does bark, I am ready as soon as she stops barking (even if it's only a quick pause) to give the quiet sign and then the good dog sign. I give a treat after the good dog sign. This helps to distract her from whatever she was barking at, which allows me to get more quiet signals practiced. It also helps to more strongly reinforce your dog for being quiet. Be sure not to give the quiet signal until she is quiet at this stage. You are teaching the dog what the quiet signal means, so you must be sure to only give it when your dog is quiet. Do this for a few weeks. Really focus on naming and rewarding those quiet times for your dog.

I am careful to always reward quiet and not to reward barking. I try not to allow my dogs to be reinforced for barking. If they are excited and barking when I come home, I wait until they quiet down before letting them out of their crates. I feed through the crate to reward the quiet, and then let them out immediately (what they really want). If they are barking at the back door, I wait for quiet before letting them out to the yard. If they are barking at meal times, I wait for quiet before feeding.

When your dog does bark, interrupt the barking. When the dog orients to you, immediately give the quiet signal. Be ready to reward quickly as soon as your dog is quiet before it can start barking again. By feeding a few treats one at a time, you can often get the dog's mind off whatever it was barking at. Keep feeding one treat right after the other at first if your dog really wants to keep barking.

As you continue to practice the quiet cue, you can gradually space out those treats to get longer periods of quiet between each one. Give the first treat right away when the dog gets quiet, and then pause for slightly longer periods of time before giving the next treat, etc. Do this step gradually. Only expect a few seconds of quiet between treats at first. If you try to move too quickly, your dog will start barking again in between treats. You can build up the time as your dog is ready. Over time, you can give fewer treats, but continuing to reward the initial quiet will help to keep the behavior strong.

If your dog barks a lot in her crate, try using a wire crate with a Manners Minder (a remote-controlled treat dispenser) put on top. The Manners Minder has a tray to catch the food that is dispensed. Remove the tray and put the machine on top of the wire crate so the food will drop through to your dog. The remote control will work from a distance, so you can release food into the crate when your dog is being quiet. Be careful to only reward when she is being quiet! Giving your dog things to keep her occupied while she is in the crate can help to keep her quiet as well.

Taking treats nicely

It's a good idea to teach your dog to take food from your fingers nicely from the very beginning. With dogs that are b/d, it is especially important. Some dogs get more excited by treats than others, but you may find that your b/d dog can smell the treats are near and will smell frantically all over the air trying to find where they are. By presenting the treats to your dog in the same way each time, you will help to avoid this a bit.

When you are offering her treats, always present them right in front of and slightly below her mouth. If she is very distracted and trying to find the treats, you can touch her lightly on the chest to get her attention downward toward your hand. Once she knows that you will always hand her the treat in the same place, she will stop the frantic searching.

Hold the treat steady, not moving it around, so she can pinpoint where the treat it. If you tease her by moving the treat all around, she may start snapping and snatching at the treat trying to catch it before it gets away. She may snatch at your fingers by mistake and that will hurt.

Feeding a treat from on top of your open palm is the safest way not to get your fingers nibbled. This is a great way to start giving treats to puppies and new dogs that haven't been taught to take food nicely yet.

To work on this skill, place a treat on top of your open palm. If you wrap your hand closed around the treat and leave just a small opening at the end of your hand, you can encourage your dog to lick at the treat through the opening. This will teach her to use her tongue and lips to take the treat and not her teeth. As she begins to take the treat more gently, you can open your hand more and more and try holding it in your fingers. Just remember to hold it steady so she doesn't need to snap at it.

When I first brought Treasure home, she would not eat treats. She was interested in the smell, but when I offered her the treat, she quickly went the other way. It took me awhile to realize that when her nose bumped into my hand, she thought there was a barrier there, so she turned around and went the other way. But when I would touch Treasure somewhere on her body first, she would then eat the treat.

She had to learn that there were different kinds of touching and that she would do different kinds of bumping. Now she very enthusiastically takes treats very gently from my fingers, even if she does bump her nose first on my hand. But in the beginning, she had never had people offering her treats, so it was a different sensation for her to have my hand so close to her nose and she thought she was going to run into something.

Off

The off cue can signal your dog to stop jumping on people, or to get off of an object (furniture for example) and onto the floor. This is a situation where I would teach the cue at the same time as I was teaching the behavior. If my dog has already jumped on me, I will most likely need to touch her in some way to get her off.

Decide what your touch cue will be. I use a flat hand pressed lightly onto the top of Treasure's head. Give the touch cue and then immediately help your dog to put all four feet back on the floor. Do this rather quickly but gently. Don't let her linger on you once you give the off cue.

Once she has all four feet on the floor, pet and reward her there, with all four feet still on the floor. If she tries to jump again, repeat the off cue and then help her get off. You must remember to pet and praise once she is on the floor. You can also hold one hand hooked in her collar once she is on the floor, to keep her down on the floor while you pet her if she is getting too excited.

Any time your dog comes to you or you go to her and she has all four feet on the floor, take time to pet and reward her for that. If all the great attention comes to her when she has all four on the floor, then that will become her position of choice.

You may choose a different cue for getting off a piece of furniture when told, or use the same one. Give the touch cue and then immediately help your dog off the furniture safely. You can use a food treat to lure her back onto the floor. Just remember that the cue should be given first, and then lure her quickly to the floor. Pet and reward her only once she has all four feet back on the floor. This can also be taught by luring the dog off the furniture a few times and then adding the cue later once she is getting off easily for the treat.

To wake up gently

There is a myth that b/d dogs are dangerous because they will always bite when they are startled or woken up. Could this ever happen? Yes, it could. But it could also happen with a dog that can see and hear. Does it happen a lot? No. Most b/d dogs are no threat when startled. Can this scenario be prevented? You can certainly lower the risk of this ever happening with your dog.

You can teach your b/d dog to wake up easily and happily. By teaching this skill to your new dog, you can prevent any issues from developing. Start training when your dog is awake and is aware of you near her. Touch your dog and then pop a wonderful treat into her mouth immediately. Don't wait to see what your dog will do. There should be no lag time. Just touch and pop the treat into her mouth. Make these really special treats. You want your dog to really look forward to being touched.

Repeat this pattern of touch and treat many times quickly in succession. Then touch your dog and pause for just a moment before giving the treat. The sequence will become – touch, dog looks expectantly for treat, and then feed. Don't pause too long, just long enough for your dog to show you that she knows the treat should come next.

In future sessions, touch different parts of your dog's body. One touch equals one treat. As your dog becomes more tolerant of you touching various parts of her body, sneak in a random touch now and then when your dog is not expecting it. Be ready with that treat immediately. Be sure to continue to use great treats every time you touch her. The more you reward the touching, the better your dog's response will be when she is surprised or woken up suddenly. You cannot do this exercise too much as long as you are rewarding every touch.

There may be times when your dog gets startled by a touch when you don't have a food treat immediately handy. Try to minimize these as much as you can, but if it happens, be ready to reward your dog with something else she likes – a small game or lots of petting if your dog enjoys that. Being woken up or startled should always mean good stuff for your dog!

When your dog is sleeping, though, be respectful. Don't wake your dog up unless it's necessary. When you do need to wake her up, do it gently. Walk heavier as you approach your dog so she can begin to feel the vibrations through the floor. When you get close to her, you can blow on her gently to wake her up. If your dog is lying on a blanket, you can wiggle the edge of the blanket to gently shake her awake. If your dog is still asleep, you can progress to brushing her gently with your hand. It is best to touch your dog on her body, not her face. That's just for safety in case she does wake up with a startle. Your hand will be away from her mouth.

Be prepared for a startle if your dog is sleeping soundly. Startling is a normal response. Just make sure that you are quickly offering your dog something wonderful! Usually the dog will recover immediately once she recognizes that it is you, and when you offer something tasty to eat, she will forget all about being startled. Be aware that your b/d dog may need you to use your hands to steady her as she wakes up. She may be disoriented as she wakes up suddenly and may jump up and bump into things nearby. Maintaining a firm but gentle touch to her body will let her know you are there while you offer the food right near her nose.

Remember that startling is a normal response. You will probably not ever get rid of it completely. But you can diminish how much the startle bothers your dog by rewarding frequently. And with lots of practice, you may notice your dog waking up easier and easier each time!

Handling and restraint games

Handling and restraint will be a huge part of your dog's life. It's important to teach her to accept touching all over her body, and to allow herself to be restrained when necessary. Most dogs don't like being reached for. If your b/d dog has any vision at all, you may notice this more. Being reached for can seem like a threatening movement from your dog's perspective unless she's been taught to see it as a positive thing. Even if your dog cannot see, she will still not appreciate being touched or grabbed suddenly. You need to teach your dog that being reached for and touched is a positive thing.

If your dog has any vision at all, begin by gently reaching toward her and offering a treat with the other hand. It's not necessary to actually touch her at this stage. This step will teach your dog that the motion of you reaching leads to a good thing. If you practice this often enough with great treats, your dog should start to approach you as she sees you reach. As she becomes comfortable with you reaching in her direction, begin to reach so that your hand comes closer and closer to her until you are actually touching her. Don't worry about grabbing or catching your dog at this point. Just focus on making the reach and the touch a good thing. Make it a game – reach and treat, touch and treat.

With a dog that cannot see, you won't need to focus so much on the reaching because she won't see your hand coming. But it will be important to practice with giving good treats each time you suddenly touch your dog. Touch your dog and immediately offer a treat right in front of her nose. Don't make her smell around for the treat. Feed the treat directly to her and feed it quickly so she associates the treat with the sudden touch. With practice, she will start to look around at your touch expectantly, waiting for a treat instead of startling and trying to run away.

When you and your dog are enjoying this game, start to vary how you reach. Sometimes reach faster and feed, sometimes touch a little bit harder and feed, touch different parts of your dog's body and feed. Always keep this game positive. If you touch a certain part of her body and she doesn't like it, feed anyway and then touch a part of her body that you know she is ok with. Work your way back to the part she wasn't sure about gradually and randomly until she feels more comfortable.

You can progress to touching your dog for longer periods of time, then holding various body parts – at first for just a moment, but then for longer periods of time. Using firm gentle pressure is often comforting to dogs, rather than a light tickling touch. Remember to work gradually and try to end the lesson while your dog is still having fun.

This will one day be your safety net. You will need to grab and get hold of your dog quickly. If you've done your homework and played these handling games, your dog will allow you to catch her easily and will look forward to whatever comes next. Continue to play handling games throughout your dog's life. Move fast and slow and reach from various angles. Keep it fun and always use great treats!

You can use these handling games to teach more advanced skills as well. Practice more in-depth exams on your dog. Check each toenail and in between her foot pads, check her teeth and open her mouth, check her ears – and after each part of the exam, pop great treats in her mouth. Practice holding her still for longer periods of time to prepare for veterinary examinations and blood draws. Try to release her while she is being still and calm if possible, but don't hold on until she panics or you will undo all the good training you've already done. Just work for shorter periods of time at first, so you can release her while she is still calm. If your dog will need special grooming or clipping routines, prepare her for them ahead of time by practicing and making each part a positive experience.

If you have a small or medium-sized dog, teach her to allow you to pick her up. When you are carrying your dog, don't let her dangle. Hold her securely and against your body so she feels supported and safe. Try to let her go at times when she is calm and still. If you are concerned about being able to hold your dog safely when she is wiggling, start by holding her in your lap while you sit on the floor. When you first start to pick her up, just lift her an inch off the floor and immediately put her down again. Work gradually. When you are placing your dog back on the floor, don't let her jump or flail around. Hold her securely and against your body until she settles down. Then slowly place her down with all four feet on the floor before letting go of her.

Taking her by the collar

This is something that we instinctively try to do – grab and steer our dog by the collar. But this is another thing that most dogs don't like unless they have been taught to accept it.

Begin with the handling games above. Then progress to touching your dog's neck and giving a treat. Then touch her collar and treat. Progress gradually to grabbing her collar, holding it for longer periods of time, pulling just enough to create pressure on the collar, steering her to move a step with you, then two steps, etc. Add variables – grab the collar more quickly and from various angles, etc. Take it slowly and your dog will soon come to expect that you grabbing her collar is a good thing that will lead to yummy goodies!

This is also the first step of teaching your dog to walk nicely on a leash!

Grooming

Grooming is a part of everyday life and it goes much smoother if you take the time to teach your dog to accept it. I always let my b/d dog smell each grooming tool before I begin to use it. The first few times, this won't mean much to your dog, but with consistency she will learn what each tool smells like and how it is used.

Begin by letting your dog smell her brush. Then use the brush on her body for one stroke and give a treat. You can progress to brushing with more strokes between treats and to brushing on different parts of her body. With a long-haired dog, you will need to progress to more in depth brushing, and not just brushing the surface hair. The same process can be used with combs and other hair removal grooming tools. Some dogs will accept grooming right away and others may need more training.

It's important to keep your dog well groomed so there is no pain involved with matted hair pulling her skin. That can be very painful and if the grooming process is painful, she won't want to cooperate. If you're starting out with a badly matted dog, it may be kinder to clip those matted areas. She may look a bit funny, but hair will grow back with time.

During the grooming session, you can use one hand to gently massage or scratch your dog in her favorite spots as you groom with the other. If you have a helper who can pet gently while you groom, that's even better, but not all of us have this luxury. Remember your dog can't hear your voice soothing and praising her, so you will need to stop and pet her now and then. This may mean interrupting the flow of your grooming session, but it is worth it to keep your dog calm and cooperative.

You may need to teach your dog various body positions to groom her properly. She may need to stand for certain parts, lay down for others, turn around, stand on a grooming table, etc. Try to spend some time familiarizing your dog with these positions before you attempt them during an actual grooming session.

As with any training, try to end the grooming session on a positive note while your dog is still calm and cooperative. You can do grooming spread out over several sessions. There is no rule saying that you must accomplish everything at one sitting. This can be especially important when clipping your dog's toenails. In the beginning, just clipping one nail and ending on a good note is a great idea. The next day, clip the next nail, etc. Just remember which nails you've already clipped!

Play and Keeping Busy

Enrichment

It's easy for life to become the same old routine for a dog that is blind and deaf. It's important for any dog to be offered new and varied things to do each day. It keeps her mind sharp and helps to keep her content. A b/d dog is missing out on stimulation which would come through her missing senses. She's not going to see or hear things happening around her to draw her interest. So, it will be up to you to provide her with interesting things to explore every day.

Offering new experiences is important to keep minds occupied and busy. Physical exercise is important, but keeping a dog's mind busy will also help to keep her content. The more new things you can expose your dog to, the more accepting she will become of new things that she will encounter in her daily life.

If these activities are new to your dog, she may not respond to them right away, or she may even avoid them in the beginning. That's ok. Dogs have preferences just like we do, and that activity may not be the right one for your dog. But, also be aware that dogs often try to avoid something new that they don't understand. It may be that with repeated exposure, your dog will start to experiment with some of the activities that she previously didn't pay any attention to.

Some enrichment activities will require you to stay nearby and supervise to keep your dog safe. Others can be activities for your dog to do when you have to leave her home alone. Switch them up. Newness is exciting to dogs. Variety is the spice of life! Try to give your dog something new to discover and try at least several times a week. You may be surprised at her reactions!

Here are some ideas to try:

Some dogs respond to the vibrations of different types of music. Treasure will often come lay by the computer when I have music playing from it. Be aware that soft and calm music will be calming to your dog. Don't leave wild and crazy music playing when you have to leave your dog home alone unless you want her to be wild and crazy while you're gone!

Putting new and different obstacles in the yard for your dog to explore can keep her busy for a while. Use obstacles that will be safe for her, and supervise her time exploring in case you need to intervene. Some ideas for new obstacles: use PVC or Styrofoam pool noodles for her to step over, a small wading pool can be empty or have a couple inches of water inside, a tunnel to walk through, or hang some paper streamers from a doorway or other threshold for her to walk through.

Some other ideas for obstacles and surfaces: a cardboard box lid, large pillows and cushions, a metal grate or screen on the ground, foil, bubble wrap, a cookie sheet, plastic tarp, woodchips, fake grass carpet, sand, gravel, mulch (be sure it is safe for dogs), bricks or paving stones, fleece, etc. Each of these gives your dog new tactile information. Let her wander over the surface or obstacle over and over again and watch her compare it to the normal surface. Don't force your dog to interact with new surfaces or obstacles. Bring her close to it and allow her to explore. You can put a few treats on or near the new thing to create a trail for her to follow, but let it be her idea. No forcing! This is supposed to be fun for your dog!

Rotate the toys you leave out for your dog. This will keep her interest peaked. It's similar to putting some of a child's unwanted toys into the closet for a rainy day. When you get them back out, it's like they are new toys all over again! Every few days, swap out groups of toys or bones. Vary the games you play with your dog as well, for the same reason.

Some dogs enjoy the air that blows from fans. Keep her safety in mind. A blind dog cannot see where the fan and cords are to avoid them and may knock the fan down on top of herself. You can put the fan behind a gate or pen so she can still feel the air, but not get right up to the fan. Try varying speeds and still vs. oscillating settings. See which your dog prefers.

All dogs enjoy sniffing new smells. Watch your dog when you get home from visiting somewhere new and she takes a long time to smell your shoes or clothes. You can introduce new smells into your dog's life by using spices and extracts from your kitchen, using an orange peel and different food smells, herb smells, etc. Be sure that your dog cannot ingest anything dangerous to her. A food such as orange peel can be put into a plastic container with a lid that has holes in it to let the odor out but prevents her from eating the peel.

You can rub a washcloth onto a new animal or scent as well. Your dog may enjoy smelling rabbits, cats, other dogs, goats, sheep, etc. If you can't bring her to the actual animal safely, you can bring the animal's scent to her. Be careful not to let your dog eat the washcloth! Remember that a dog's sense of smell is very developed. Don't just shove the new scent into her face. Place the scent near her for her to discover on her own. Then she can get as close to it as she chooses in her own time without being overwhelmed.

If your dog likes to dig, provide her with a digging pit. You can hide new toys and treats there every day to give her an acceptable place to dig and explore.

If your dog can see lights, she may enjoy exploring a box with Christmas tree lights taped to it. Try solid lights and blinking lights. Don't let her chew the cords!

Take special time every day to sit and touch your dog. It will give you some special time together, but touch is also calming for both you and your dog and it offers your dog's nervous system important input. Petting and stroking with love and intention will do both of you good. If you know how, adding Healing Touch for Animals®, TTouch®, massage or other bodywork will also be beneficial for your dog's well-being.

Taking your dog to new places and to meet new people can help keep her life exciting. Think of all the new smells and sensations of going out some place new! A smaller dog can ride in a stroller or wagon, or even be carried to help keep her safe. Take your dog on walks. Go to a new park and let your dog explore safely on a long leash or in an ex pen with you supervising. Take her on car rides to run short errands. All of these involve your dog being able to smell new smells and experience new sensations.

Playtime!

Safety: Just a few words about safety for you and others while playing with your b/d dog. A dog that cannot see may throw her head out to grab for a toy or other items, or even try to reach for you while playing, and bite down on you instead without realizing it. You may need to modify how you play with your b/d dog to keep it safe for both of you. Your dog may have trouble realizing where your hand ends and the toy begins when she's excited in the middle of a fun game. This can be especially important to take into account when playing tug games. Tug games can be great interactive games to play with your b/d dog, but you will need to pay a bit of extra attention to protect your hands and fingers from accidental bites. Choose long tug toys so you can hold one end and offer her the other end. The more room between your hand and her mouth, the better!

Toys: B/d dogs enjoy toys too! What your dog will like is an individual thing. There are as many types of dog toys as you can imagine. Use whatever your dog likes and is safe for her. If your dog is chewing up and eating pieces of toys, those are not safe toys for her to use.

There are scented dog toys or you can create your own. You can put various odors onto stuffed and fabric toys and tugs to make them more interesting for your dog. Place the odor in a Ziploc bag with the toy overnight so the toy will absorb the odor. There are stuffed toys with pouches in them to hide food or squeaky discs. You can put food in them to entice your dog to play with them. There are many types of food dispensing toys and puzzles now being made for dogs. These are usually washable and fairly durable. These are usually very popular with all dogs!

When using toys that hold food, be careful about allowing multiple dogs in the area together. Some dogs can get possessive of their food around other dogs and your b/d dog will be at a disadvantage. If you have multiple dogs in your home, they can each have a food toy in different rooms of the house, or in their crates, or while separated by gates to keep everyone safe.

If your dog has limited vision, bigger toys may be easier for her to see than smaller ones, or ones with contrasting colors rather than neutral colors that blend with surroundings. Your dog may be able to see a ball that glows in the dark or one with a blinking light in a dimly lit room.

If your dog can hear, try toys that make different noises. Not just a squeaky toy, but try toys that rattle or have a bell inside that will continue to make a noise as it rolls. Some toys make silly noises as they bounce, too. Your dog may be able to follow the sound to chase the toy.

While your b/d dog won't be able to see the toys move or hear them make noises, she can still learn to enjoy playing with toys. Some toys and balls vibrate. Your dog may be intrigued by these. Using food dispenser toys will probably be popular once you teach her how to use them. Hard rubber toys often have a scent added to them and usually have at least one hole in them. You can put a bit of peanut butter inside the hole so your dog learns to smell out the toy. Start by teasing your dog a bit with the toy and then dropping it very close to your dog so she feels the thump and then smells the peanut butter in the toy. Let her lick the toy a bit and wiggle it around to keep her excited about it. Then drop it a bit farther away, but not so far that she can't find it easily. Over time, she may learn to sniff out the toy farther and farther away.

When encouraging your dog to return to you with the toy, keep in mind that she can't see you. Stay in the same place so she knows where to return to you. Patting the floor may help to encourage her back to you, and you can use the come cue once you've taught it to her.

Tug games can be fun to play with your dog as long as you take precautions to keep it safe. Don't let the game get too crazy ... that's when accidental bites are likely to occur. Gently moving the tug toy back and forth and playing gentle tug games can be a nice way to interact with your dog. To get her to grab the tug toy, pull it across her paws so it makes contact with her and she can tell where it is. Use a long tug toy so you can keep lots of distance between her mouth and your hand.

Teach her to let go when you give her a cue to give or when you stop moving the toy. You can teach this by giving the cue and then immediately offering a treat right next to your dog's nose. As she lets go of the toy to get the treat, you can switch to petting and rewarding her with the treat. Over time, she will start to anticipate the treat is coming when you give the cue. Eventually you won't need the treat every time, but you can have her give the toy, pet to reward, and then start the game again.

Games: There are many fun games you can play with your b/d dog. Here are a few of my favorites:

Treat scatter game: This is a fun game and is very simple for you. It can be played inside or outside, each one offering its own fun and challenges. Take a portion of your dog's meal and toss it up into the air so it lands scattered all over the ground. Let your dog spend some time sniffing out all the food.

Food trails: Create trails of varying lengths, with turns if you wish, using a portion of your dog's meal. Then take her to one end of the trail and let her sniff out each piece of food. This can be done inside or outside, just make sure the trail does not lead her to some place that isn't safe. You might even leave the rest of her meal in a food toy or puzzle at the end of the trail.

Scent trails: Your dog may like to follow trails made with scents (with or without food along the trail). Try using kitchen extracts or other new and interesting odors. Start with short trails and then progress to longer ones with turns.

Finding hidden treats: Use a portion of your dog's meal – are you seeing a pattern here? By using your dog's meal for these games, you won't be adding too many treats or calories to your dog's diet and risking stomach upset. Start with very easy finds, even putting the food near her in the middle of the floor. Gradually move the treats to harder places as your dog learns the game. This can also be played inside or outside.

Hide and seek: You can hide and let your dog find you. If your dog needs some incentive to come find you, you can hide while holding her dinner bowl or some yummy treats that smell too good to resist. Start easy while you're teaching her this game.

Muffin tin game: Place food in the cups of a muffin tin. Then place a tennis ball or other toy inside each muffin cup on top of the food. Let your dog discover how to remove the toys to get to the food. At first, you may need to help her by moving the toys slightly so she gets the idea to push them out of the way. Try bigger or smaller toys to make the game easier or more difficult for your dog. It's best to place the muffin tin on a non-slip mat or to hold it to prevent it from sliding across the floor while your dog plays.

The shell game: Use three cups or flower pots with a hole in the bottom and turn them upside down. Put a treat under one of the cups (yogurt cups work well for this). Let your dog smell the cups to find which one has the treat under it.

Fitness and exercise: It's important to keep your dog's body healthy as well as her mind. Some b/d dogs need help staying in shape because they are less likely to run around and play on their own.

Running and playing with other dogs can be great exercise if your dog will do this and you have a safe place to allow her to run. Always use caution when allowing your b/d dog to greet new dogs. Have both dogs on leash and introduce them slowly. It is safest to let your b/d dog play with one or two other compatible dogs in a safely enclosed area while always being supervised. Dog parks may not be a safe place to let your b/d dog play. Proceed with caution.

Swimming is great exercise. Again be sure to keep your dog safe. If you are at a lake or other body of water, keep your b/d dog on leash for her safety. She won't be able to hear or see you calling her back and she may become disoriented while out in the water and need help to get back to you. Always supervise your dog around water. Dogs can swim in swimming pools too, but again, be careful to always supervise so you can help your dog find the steps when she gets tired. Take the time to teach your dog to swim gradually. Don't just assume she likes the water or can swim. Get in the water with her and help her feel comfortable. You should consider getting your dog a life jacket created for dogs that fits her well. That way she can have fun and you can have more peace of mind. Even with a life jacket, you should still always supervise your dog around water. Dogs can drown quickly.

Going for walks is a popular way to give a dog exercise. Walking down the street can offer your dog many new smells and places to explore, but will also bring many challenges. You must watch out for your dog constantly. Your eyes and ears automatically give your body cues of things to watch out for, but you may not be conscious of this happening. Things like curbs, sign posts, fire hydrants, branches from bushes, someone coming towards you, another dog approaching, children reaching for her, traffic coming, a hole in the sidewalk – these are all things that you must watch out for to warn your dog or steer her around safely. Always keep your dog on leash during walks.

If you walk in areas with lots of traffic or with big trucks, you may notice your dog freezing and acting confused. She probably feels the strong vibrations through the ground and the air surrounding high traffic areas and has become disoriented. Help her gently to know which way to go. If you walk in these areas often, she will get used to the vibrations, but be ready to help her when she needs it.

In quieter areas, you may want to allow your b/d dog to explore and wander. Get her a long leash or use a clothesline attached to her collar. Remember that your dog relies on you for her safety. If you can't reach her quickly, you cannot keep her safe. A long leash will allow you to keep her safe.

There are inflatable balance discs, balls, peanuts, and other equipment, that can be helpful for keeping your b/d dog in shape. These keep your dog's core muscles strong and flexible. There are various videos available that show different activities to do with your dog using this equipment. Always supervise your dog during these activities. The equipment should not be left with your dog when you aren't actively using it with your dog.

Teaching
Basic Commands

Target stick

The idea of a target stick is that the dog learns to watch and follow the stick (which is acting as a target). The stick can then be used to teach your dog new behaviors. Obviously a b/d dog will not be able to see the stick, but we can modify the concept of the stick to encourage your dog to follow it.

A long-handled wooden spoon with peanut butter, baby food meats, or another sticky and smelly food on it can come in handy when teaching various behaviors. When working with a small dog, you can use the spoon to lead your dog into position without bending over excessively.

When using food on a spoon, there isn't much training that needs to be done. Let your dog lick the food from the spoon. Then move the spoon a short distance away and let her smell her way to it so she can get another lick. Move the spoon slowly ahead of her as she learns to follow behind it. Offer her licks of the spoon now and then to keep her motivated and offer rewards for appropriate behavior.

If you wanted to take this idea further, you could tape a scented cotton pad to the end of a dowel rod and teach your dog to follow that. You would need to pair the scented stick with food to make it valuable to your dog. Then you could reduce the food that was on the stick until you were using only the scented pad. And you could reward with food from your hand as the reward. If you choose to use a scented stick, be sure the scent you choose is only used for the purpose of having your dog follow something. Smelling that same scent at other times may be confusing for your dog if she thinks she needs to follow it. When using scents for training cues, it is also important to keep the scent isolated and away from your dog when you're not using it. Keeping it sealed in a plastic bag or two and storing it in a room where your dog doesn't spend time is a good idea.

Some dogs have personal space issues and dislike being touched. Food on a spoon can be helpful for moving a dog around the house or yard that has issues being touched, or that is distrustful in the beginning. It can be handy to use food on a spoon to help teach leash leading exercises if your dog is very short.

Target sticks are also very useful for teaching tricks and even everyday behaviors. Teaching your dog to turn in a circle can be easier if she's following the spoon with food. You may find the spoon helpful in teaching your dog to do stairs or in stepping up and down curbs. Use your imagination.

If your dog is able to see well enough, you can attach a ball to one end of a stick to make it easier for her to see. Experiment with using a light colored ball or a darker one. Which one is easier for her to see? A bigger ball may be easier for her to see than a smaller one.

All done/release

It's important when you begin to use cues to ask your dog to do something that you also have a cue that lets your dog know she is finished doing what you asked. This is the release cue. When you ask your dog to sit, your dog doesn't know if you want her to sit forever, or just for a second, or if she can just wander off whenever she wants to. You are giving the sit behavior a beginning (the sit cue) and you need to give it an end as well (the release cue).

To teach the release cue, give the cue you've chosen, and then do something to entice your dog to move out of the position she was in. So, from the sit position, give the release cue and then entice your dog to stand up and move. You can lure her to take a step or two forward or you can lead her gently forward with her collar. Use the same release cue to end each behavior. If you always help your dog to move after the release cue, she will learn it quickly.

During the stage when you are still using the lure, remember to reward the actual behavior (sit) while she is still in position. Once she's done eating, give the release cue. Lure her to move if you need to and then feed once she moves out of the sit position. Basically you are teaching and rewarding two behaviors – the sit and the release.

When you no longer need the lure to get the behavior, still reward (good dog signal) while your dog is in position. Then release her from the exercise. You should still continue to reward with food sometimes as this keeps your dog's enthusiasm high. We all want to be paid with something valuable for our efforts and your dog is no different. Save the food rewards for your dog's best efforts and she will continue to try harder for you.

Sit

There are several ways to teach your dog to sit on cue. Choose the one that works best with your dog. Keep in mind that it will be most helpful to your dog if you reward while she is still in the sit position. You may need to pet her while holding her in position and feeding at first until she gets the idea to stay sitting.

You can use a marker signal to capture the sit behavior. When your dog sits on her own, mark the behavior and reward. In order for this to work, you will need to be close by and have treats always available. The marker signal must happen as your dog is sitting, and the reward must follow immediately after. If your dog sits a lot on her own, this could be a good method for you to use. If you are having trouble teaching your dog to sit with other methods, and you see her do a lovely sit on her own, if you have treats handy, you can mark it and then reward. This might help her get the idea that sitting is something that you like her to do. Your other sit training may then progress a little faster.

You may be able to lure your dog into a sit position. Hold the treat directly above your dog's nose so she can reach up her nose easily to sniff it. The important part is to keep the treat very close to her nose without letting her get the treat. Slowly move the treat upward to stretch her nose up and back toward her shoulders. As her head stretches upward, her rear end should sink down towards the floor.

Immediately when her rear reaches the floor, pet/mark and give a treat. If you can get the treat to her while she is still sitting, progress will be faster. Each time you lead her into a sit, it should get easier and easier as she learns that the behavior will lead to a treat.

This makes it sound very easy, but in reality, many variables can happen along the way. If your dog starts to sit but always pops back into a stand, you may need to reward just the beginning of the sit at first. As her rear starts to sink down just a little bit, pet and give the treat. Over time, you will begin to see her rear going lower and lower towards the floor. Reward these lower movements and stop rewarding the ones that aren't so low. Eventually you will have a sit!

With active and wiggly dogs, it may be difficult to get her to stay in place as you try to lure her into the sit. You can help by positioning her with her rear towards a corner to help guide her to stand still, and put one hand gently under her chin or on her chest, while you lead her nose with the treat in the other hand.

When you can easily lure your dog into a sit position, begin to add the cue. Give the sit cue and then immediately help her with the lure to sit. Reward her while she's in position, and then remember to give a release cue to let her know that repetition is finished. With time, you can give the sit cue and then pause to see if your dog will begin to respond on her own without the lure. Be ready to help her if she is confused. But lure her less and less until she is responding on her own to the sit cue. Remember to reward in the sit position and then give the release cue so she knows she can get up.

If your dog has enough vision, the hand motion of luring her into a sit can be used as the sit cue. Just fade having food in your hand and the movement of your hand up over her head will become the signal for her to sit.

If these other techniques don't work, you can try gently molding your dog's body into position. This is how I taught Treasure to sit. I held her gently in place with one hand on her chest under her chin. With the other hand, I stroked gently down her back and scooped under her rear (on the outside of her tail) to gently press the back of her rear legs. This caused her to bend her rear legs into a sit position. I only expected a slight bend of her legs at first and rewarded that. As her body became more flexible, I allowed more of a bend until she was actually sitting.

Once I had her sitting, I held her in the sit position gently while petting and feeding her. I held her in position so she would associate the petting and reward with the position of being in the sit. I then released her and let her stand up, which allowed me to start another repetition. Each time, she sat quicker and quicker with less help from me.

At that point, I started to add the sit cue before helping her to sit. I gave the sit cue and then quickly helped her into the sit position. After several repetitions, I noticed her starting to sit on her own when I gave the sit cue before I could actually help her into position. Over several more sessions, she learned to respond to only the cue and I no longer had to help her into the sit position. I also was able to hold her in position less and less as I pet and fed her. She learned to hold the position on her own.

Down

There are several ways to teach your dog to lie down. Choose the one that works best with your dog. Keep in mind that it will be most helpful to your dog if you reward while she is in the down position.

Probably the easiest way to teach your dog to lie down is by using a food lure. Begin with your dog in a sit position. Lure your dog's nose down toward the floor between her front legs. Keep the food right by her nose but don't let her eat it. Move the food slowly so she follows it with her nose. At first, just reward your dog for dipping her nose downward toward the floor. After a repetition or two of this, you should find that your dog is following the lure downward more quickly and fluidly. At this point, continue the lure downward a bit more. Watch for your dog's front legs to step forward and her shoulders to drop down following her nose toward the floor. At this point, reward. Gradually lure your dog down closer to the ground. The ultimate goal is that your dog will lie down completely onto her elbows before getting the reward.

Sometimes your dog may need a little bit more help than just the lure. Try to lure your dog's nose under a low obstacle. You can use a chair, coffee table, or even your own legs. As your dog follows the treat under the obstacle, she will naturally lower her neck and shoulders and will often begin to crawl under the obstacle, ending in a down position.

You can also gently place your dog into a down from a sit position. Gently lifting and sliding her front feet forward, may allow you to guide her to the floor into a down position. Don't just drop her into a down. Use your body to ease her to the floor. Reward while she is lying down. Once she starts to get the idea, you need to help her less and less, so she gets the idea to go down on her own, not just to let you lift her down.

You can also capture the down by rewarding your dog any time she lies down on her own. By rewarding the down position, you will begin to see her lying down more often in the hopes of getting rewarded. By watching your dog closely, you will begin to anticipate when she will lie down and you can then introduce the cue. For example, if your dog has a favorite dog bed, be ready when she is starting to lie down and give the down cue when you are sure she is going to do it. Then reward once she's down.

Once you are able to get your dog to go into a down position easily, you can begin to introduce a cue. Give the cue right before you help your dog lay down. Then reward while keeping your dog in the down position. After she is finished eating, give your release cue and help her move out of position. You can use the hand motion of the lure to the floor as a visual cue if your dog has enough vision to follow it.

Repeat this sequence for a few sessions. Then give the cue and pause just for a short moment to see if she starts to respond on her own without your help. Be ready to step in and help quickly so the flow is not interrupted, and be sure to reward once she's down. Over time you will need to help her less and less, but continue to reward once she is down. Don't forget your release cue to let her know the exercise is finished.

Walk on leash/heel

The first step in teaching your b/d dog to walk on a leash is to teach her to respond to collar cues. If you've been playing handling and taking by the collar games, you've got a good head start. If you haven't started playing those games yet, begin there. Your dog needs to know that you touching and steering her by the collar is a good thing before you can proceed.

Once your dog is comfortable with you holding her collar, begin to keep your hand on her collar for longer periods of time before rewarding. Pull slightly on the collar and then feed a treat. Don't expect her to move with you at first, just put a small amount of pressure on the collar and then reward her. Apply the pressure in all directions while you are teaching this step. Once your dog accepts this, begin to maintain the pressure in one direction for a bit longer until she takes a very small step to come along in the direction of the pressure. Immediately when you notice this small step, release the pressure on the collar and reward her.

With time and patience, build this up slowly until you can lead her by the collar in any direction just by applying gentle pressure in the direction you want her to go. Don't pull her with you. If you try to pull a b/d dog with you, she may panic. You are pulling her into the darkness where she has no idea what will appear in her path. It has to be her choice to trust you and to come along with the pressure. Always be aware of where you are leading your dog so that you won't run her into anything. For her to want to come with you, she needs to trust you.

Once you can lead your dog easily by just a small pressure cue on her collar, you are ready to add the leash. A leash is not for pulling your dog around or controlling her. A leash is for safety and to use as a communication tool with your dog. By putting a leash on your dog, you are limiting her options for acting in ways that dogs would normally act. Often, we use a leash as an excuse to require our dogs to be on our agenda. It's easy to not pay as much attention to a dog's attempts to communicate with you when she is on a leash because in your mind, you think she is safe and being controlled by you.

We often use leashes to pull our dogs closer to things that scare them than they would normally go on their own. We expect them to deal with being wherever we want them to be. But for many dogs, being on a leash creates stress and anxiety because we are preventing them from acting in ways that are comfortable and safe to them. This is why I take so much time to introduce the leash properly. I want it to be a safe and positive piece of equipment for my dogs. They will need to wear leashes in most situations outside of my home for safety purposes. I want them to be confident and happy when wearing leashes.

When you first attach the leash to your dog, let her feel the weight of it on her collar. Don't go anywhere. Let her sniff the leash as you attach it and then just sit together. Pet her and feed her some treats. Some dogs will be ok with this step from the beginning. Others may need a few sessions of learning that the new sensation of a leash is a good thing. Once you can connect the leash and your dog doesn't show any concern, you can begin leading her.

When you first start leading with the leash attached, hold the leash in the hand farthest from your dog so you can use the closest hand to lead her by the collar. This is a known behavior to her (leading by the collar) but now with the added aspect of the leash being attached.

Keep this fun for your dog with petting and lots of treats. Begin to slide your hand from the collar to the snap of the leash. Now you are beginning to lead her with gentle pressure on the leash. By moving your hand slowly, your dog can get used to the gradual changes in how the pressure feels. It feels a bit different to be led directly from a collar than to be led from a leash. Again, keep it your dog's choice to walk with you. Never force her and drag her with the leash.

If she stops and won't walk with you, you should stop too and maintain the gentle pressure in the direction you want to go. Just stop and wait. When you feel even the slightest movement in your direction, release the pressure and praise your dog. Then begin again. If you get frustrated and pull her, she will put on the brakes and begin fighting the leash. If you wait patiently for her to take that one step, she will have made the decision to come with you and her confidence will grow with each success.

You should be able to progress to sliding your hand more and more up the leash until you can stand up and lead her gently with the leash. I use various leash cues. Gentle pressure in a certain direction means that we are going forward, turning or stopping. A loose leash that is wiggled means I need her attention now and we are moving on. I usually use this when we are on a leisurely walk and I am letting her sniff. When I need more precision and want to keep her near me, I will often use a solid leash.

Your dog will be able to feel each change in the leash movement. If you keep just a gentle bit of pressure on the leash, she will be able to feel where you are, how fast you're going, and when you turn and stop. If your dog wants to go one way and you want to go the other, simply stop and hold the gentle pressure until she comes back to your direction. You've already taught her to come towards that gentle pressure, so she knows that as a cue to come towards you. Now begin to walk your dog in new areas. Remember to steer her around any obstacles that are in her path.

You may find that your dog actually walks faster and with more confidence when you steer her with the collar or leash than when she's walking by herself. She trusts you not to run her into anything, so she is able to move faster. If she was walking by herself, she may need to go slower because she will need to find and avoid obstacles in her path. With you leading the way, she can weave around obstacles like they weren't even there!

Equipment cues

Just a few words about the equipment you choose to use with your b/d dog. There are harnesses, collars, head halters, flexi leashes, and so much more. Choose whatever works best for you and your dog. She will learn the differences between the various pieces of equipment.

If you are using a harness or head halter for walking your dog, just adapt the above instructions and break down your training into small steps. Using a head halter can offer you a great tool for stopping or steering a b/d dog before she can run into obstacles. Head halters are not meant to be yanked and can cause physical issues if they are used that way. They are meant to be used with gentle pressure to steer your dog. Make sure you know how to use the equipment that you choose properly.

You may find that you get better results using different pieces of equipment in different circumstances. That is fine too. Your dog will learn the different contexts in which each piece of equipment is used. For example, you may prefer to use a harness and long leash when letting your dog explore in a field, but you may prefer to use the leash attached to a head halter or regular collar when out for walks on the sidewalk. Using a body harness with a large b/d dog can provide you with a handle close to her back with which to steer her and give her cues.

One quick word about flexi leashes. If you have done a good job teaching your dog to respond to gentle pressure cues, you may find that she won't pull out on a flexi leash. This is because as the flexi leash extends, there is always gentle pressure pulling her back toward the pulley part of the leash. You may need to extend the leash and then lock it in place so there is no tension on your dog's collar. Then when you want to call her back towards you, hold the leash so it won't suddenly pull her and release the lock. With your hand on the leash, gradually allow the pressure to come back to the leash.

How to make a solid leash

A solid leash can be helpful with smaller dogs. It allows you to give subtle leash cues at your dog's neck level, which are clearer than if they come from far above her. It will also save your back from needing to stoop to give those cues.

A solid leash could be useful during walks on busy sidewalks when you will need to steer your dog around obstacles or for training exercises when you want your dog to stay right next to your leg. A solid leash is not useful for walks when you want to let your dog sniff around and explore. A regular or long leash would work better for that.

It may take some practice for you to learn how to handle the solid leash fluently. There is less slack than with a regular leash, so your cues travel directly to your dog's neck. You will need to use less leash pressure; sometimes even just a small adjustment of your hand or wrist will give a different cue to your dog.

You can use a very simple and inexpensive version of a solid leash, or you can create a very elaborate one. The solid leash I use is a curtain rod that was the right height for me to hold easily in my hand and also reached down to my dog's neck level. Getting one that was too long would be cumbersome for me to hold. Getting one that was too short would require me to bend over too far.

The curtain rod has a finished surface and has comfortable end caps on it. It has a more finished look and feel than a wooden dowel rod, which would have worked just as well. I then cut up an old leash with a small clip that wouldn't be too heavy or clunky for my dog's neck. I left a small tab of leash connected to the clip. This would allow a bit of flexibility between my dog and the rod. I then used heavy tape to attach the tab of the leash to the end of the curtain rod. Voila! This original version has worked so well for us that I haven't seen a need to change it.

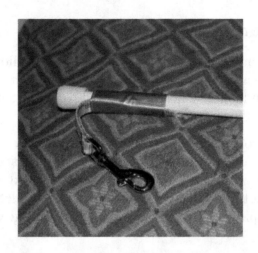

Come

To teach your dog to come when called, you will need a signal that you can give her from a distance. I use my breath to blow on Treasure. She follows my breath back to me. In different situations, I may also use other come signals. When Treasure is outside on the wooden deck or ramp, I can stomp on the deck and she knows to come to the door and come inside. In the dark, I can flash the porch light and if she is close enough to notice the flash, she will come inside. You may be able to use a long reacher or dowel rod with a padded end to touch her and lead her to you. But the one that is most useful to me wherever we are is my breath.

Begin very close to your dog and give your come signal. Don't expect her to come to you, as she doesn't know what the cue means yet. Just give the come signal and then immediately hand her a great treat. Make it something really special to motivate her. Do this often. Give the cue to come and feed. Don't expect her to do anything at this point. You just want her to associate the cue with great things.

When you can give the cue to come and she immediately startles and looks for you and the treat, you are ready to move on to the next step. Now start to give the cue when you are next to her and be ready to reward your dog for even a slight turn in your direction. Try it from both sides and even from directly behind her until she turns toward you whenever you give the cue.

Gradually, shape your dog's response so she comes farther towards you. Add distance gradually. Try it in new areas but start close up to her and then build distance again slowly. Always reward your dog when she comes to you. Never call her to you for things that she won't like – grooming, medication, confinement, corrections. If you do, she may decide not to come to you because it won't be rewarding for her.

With a dog that cannot see or hear you, it is important to continue a tactile signal until your dog gets to you. Help her know where you are in space as she learns to come to you from farther away. Reward once she gets close enough to you for you to touch her easily.

Stay

Your dog can learn to stay in different positions. Most dogs prefer to stay in the down position. It is most comfortable for the dog to stay in for a length of time. It also takes the most effort for the dog to move from a down position, as opposed to a sit or a stand stay. If you expect to teach the stay in different positions, however, you may want to teach the sit stay before the down stay. Dogs taught to down stay first, may often try to lie down while left on a sit stay because that is their habit already.

Stay can be a difficult exercise for your b/d dog to learn. All dogs like to be with us and don't necessarily like to be left behind while we walk away. But b/d dogs really like to keep track of us and they won't be able to track us with their eyes as we leave to know where we are.

Begin teaching stay by standing right next to your dog. Don't be in a hurry to walk away. When you are practicing sit and down positions, reward while your dog is in position but don't release her. Instead, quickly reward again with her still in position. By rewarding several times without a release cue, you are getting your dog used to staying in position longer. After feeding several treats, then give the release cue.

Gradually pause slightly longer between treats, so your dog learns to wait in position longer for the treats. When you are sure your dog will wait in position for the next reward to come, you can begin to add the stay cue. If she is still trying to move out of position before the release cue, you need to practice this step more before moving on.

Ask your dog to sit. Reward in position. Then give the stay cue and immediately reward your dog while she is still in the sit position. Then release. She just did her first very short sit stay! The goal will be to very gradually build up the amount of time between the stay cue and the reward. If your dog gets up after the stay cue but before the reward, begin again without rewarding. The next time, make the time between the stay cue and the reward shorter so she can be successful.

Build up to a 20 second stay with you staying right next to your dog. Make sure you aren't touching her during that time, because as you start to walk away from her, you won't be able to touch her. You don't want her relying on touching you to stay in place. Make your stay cue very clear, and make your release cue very clear. Any rewards should come while your dog is still in the stay position. If your dog lays down during the stay and you wanted her to sit, give the release cue and let her get up so you can start over again. Do not reward, but make the next sit stay shorter so you can reward while she is still sitting.

When your dog can do a 20 second stay with you next to her, you can take one small step away from her after you give the stay cue. Immediately step back next to her and reward. Each time you practice, vary the direction you step away from her. One time go out to the side, one time to the front, one time backwards. When this is going well, take two steps away and immediately come back. Then take two steps away and build up the time again to 20 seconds gradually. It's better to come back quickly and be able to reward a successful stay than to try to stretch the time too far and cause your dog to make a mistake.

Gradually add more distance and more time. When you go farther, cut down the time at first and then build back up. When you want to add more time, stay close by at first.

Leave it

I use one finger pushed down gently on top of the dog's muzzle for the leave it cue and I teach it from the beginning in this case. I begin with a rather boring item at first – a wooden block perhaps. I let my dog smell it briefly and then give the leave it cue. By giving the leave it cue, you will be encouraging her to move her nose in another direction away from the block and your finger pressure. As soon as she moves her nose away, stop the pressure on her nose and begin feeding treats. The leave it cue should come to mean for her to turn her head away from whatever she is showing interest in.

You can start rather quickly to give a shorter leave it cue and then give your dog the option of choosing to respond and turn away from the block. As soon as she turns away, begin rewarding and continue for several seconds. If she turns back to the block, give the leave it cue again and reward when she turns away from it.

Substitute other non-food items for the block and practice the leave it cue again. Make sure your dog has a good turn away response to the leave it cue on many different items. Then you can begin to use food items. Start with things that probably aren't too interesting to your dog, like a potato or an empty box that had some pasta in it. Gradually use food items that are more and more tempting to your dog. As you ask your dog to leave food alone, be sure the reward you are offering for turning away is high value.

Always prevent your dog from actually getting the food item you have told her to leave. As the food gets more tempting, she may try to grab the food anyway. Be faster than her and prevent her from getting it. As soon as she stops trying to get the food, start rewarding.

When you are confident that your dog will turn away from whatever you ask her to, give the leave it cue and don't reward immediately when she turns away. Pause just a bit before rewarding. Making that pause longer will stretch the amount of time your dog will be able to leave something alone after the cue.

You can use the leave it cue to get your dog to turn away from food, things she wants to chew, distracting smells, other animals, etc. The cue is the same. When she turns away from whatever it is, reward. Some things will be very difficult for your dog to turn away from. In those cases, have great rewards and use them frequently while your dog is leaving the item. Make it easy for her to be successful.

Wait

A wait is not the same as a stay. A stay cue means the dog should stay very still in the same position that you left her in until you release her. Wait is generally just a pause while you give other direction. I use a finger touch to the dog's forehead. The dogs learn this one on their own generally. When I am getting the dog out of the crate in the car, I use the wait cue while I get the leash attached to her collar. When there is a step or a curb and I need the dog to pause so I can give further direction, I use the wait cue. Anytime I need the dog to just hang out for a moment, I use the wait cue. Remember to tell your dog what to do next after a wait. It's not fair for her to remain waiting forever while you go off to do something else.

Stand

There may be times you want your dog to stand instead of sitting or laying down. The stand cue comes in handy for grooming, for wiping muddy paws, or for preventing your dog from sitting in a mud puddle while on a walk.

To teach your dog to stand, use a food lure right at her nose level and move it straight out away from her nose so she has to reach out to get it. Move the food slowly, enticing her to stand up to follow it. As soon as she stands, reward her. The idea is not to make her walk forward too far, just to stand up on all four legs. To assist her, you can touch lightly under her belly, right in front of her hind leg and she will usually stand up. This can become your cue and doesn't really require much teaching. This is a spot where dogs often sniff each other, and it is polite dog behavior to stand still and allow the other dogs to sniff.

You can go on to teach a stand stay if you'd like, following the instructions for teaching stay. I find it helpful to teach a sit and down stay before trying the stand stay. It's harder for a dog to stay in a stand position and not move because she is already on her feet. So it's helpful for her to already have an idea of how to stay before you expect her to stand and stay.

Other Training

Stroller, wagon

You can teach a smaller dog to ride in a stroller or wagon. I find this helpful when taking my dogs to pet expos and other crowded places. A stroller can also become a portable safe place that you can take with you anywhere you take your dog.

Make sure the stroller is the right size for your dog and that it's safe. Some strollers made for pets come with mesh panels that can be zipped up to keep your dog inside safely. If the stroller you are using does not have mesh, always keep your dog on a leash that you hold. Always be careful when using a stroller that it won't tip over.

You will want to make the stroller a place where good things happen. You may want to use a special blanket or bed in the stroller so she knows this is her spot. Feed your dog treats near the stroller, let her sniff and explore it, then while she's in the stroller pet and praise her there. Start with just a short time in the stationary stroller. Then let her hang out for longer periods of time in it. Stay near her to give her a sense of security.

Begin to move the stroller slightly back and forth while you pet and reward her. Stop and let your dog relax again in the stationary stroller. Then move it slightly again. Work for only short periods of time at first. Gradually move the stroller more, make turns, go at different paces. Different surfaces may create different vibrations in the stroller that your dog will need to get used to. Stop and reassure her if she seems worried by something.

You should never let your dog decide to jump out of the stroller on her own. Teach her to stay in it until you release her and help her get out, or until you pick her up out of it. If you let her jump out of the stroller whenever she feels like it, she could get injured.

Steps

A b/d dog can be taught to go up and down steps safely. Within her own home, she may learn to do the steps so comfortably that it is easy to forget she is b/d. It is always safest, even within her own home, to make sure she is always supervised on full flights of steps. Putting gates at the top and bottom of long flights of stairs is a good safety measure. Also, check any railing slats to be sure they are not big enough for your dog to slip or squeeze through. When traveling or visiting others with steps, keep your dog away from the steps unless you are directly supervising and helping her. It only takes one slip or wrong step for her to go tumbling down the steps and she could get injured and will most likely be scared.

It's usually easiest to teach your dog to go up the steps first because it's easier for her to judge the height of the next step. If you have access to a small set of stairs, or stairs that are broken up with landings, that is probably the easiest place to start. Once she learns to do a few stairs, doing more will be a lot easier.

Feed treats to your dog at the bottom of the steps. Get her interested in the treats. Slowly bring her closer to the bottom step and then feed the treat from the edge of the first step. When she is comfortable with this, move the treat back farther on the step away from her, but keep it on that first step. As she gets closer to the step to reach for the treat, she will touch her chest or lower legs to the front of the step. This will be important information for her. It will allow her to judge the height of the first step.

Now hold the treat in your hand again and slowly lure her head up and forward over the steps. When you can get her to stretch to the second step, begin putting the treat on the edge of the second step. Small dogs will need to step up on the first step to reach the treat. Larger dogs will need to stretch even farther over the first step and may begin to lift a leg up as they reach. Use lots of petting and feed treats to her while she remains with her feet on the first step. If she wants to jump back down to the ground, let her.

As she gets more comfortable going up the first step for the treat, you can use the same procedure to get her to climb the second step. Stay very close so you are available to help her and prevent her from slipping. As your dog eats a treat from one step, be ready with a treat to lead her to the next step. If your dog acts like she's confused or stuck, touch her and reassure her. If your dog already knows how to be led by the collar, you can use gentle pressure on the collar up and forward in the direction you want her to go. Don't pull her up the stairs. Let it be her decision to move, just suggest the movement to her with your cue. You might find that having your hand on her collar gives her enough confidence to continue moving.

Even when your dog is going up the steps on her own, you may need to help her with her collar lightly or with treats for several weeks. She will need to learn the muscle memory involved with doing the steps – how many steps there are, the height and depth of the steps, and how to get to the steps and approach them. Make sure each of her interactions with the steps is positive.

In order for your dog to come down the steps she will need to learn to balance her body in new ways with her rear end much higher than her front end. If you have only a long set of stairs to work on, you can pick your dog up (if she's not too big) and place her gently on the last few steps with her front end on the lower steps and her rear end on the higher steps. Only expect her to do a few at a time if possible. Hold her gently in place until she starts to find her balance. Then progress to helping her down the last few steps.

Coming down the steps can be harder because your dog won't be able to feel the depth or height of the drop off. Sitting next to your dog on the step may let you help her easier. Use treats and very slowly ask her to stretch farther and farther down the steps. Keep the treat very close to the steps, not out in the air. It can often help to get your dog laying down right at the edge of the top step so she can feel the drop off with her foot. Many b/d dogs stretch their foot down first to feel where the next step begins before committing to going down the stairs.

It may help to sit on the step below your dog and in front of her so she can smell you there. By moving yourself down one step at a time, you may be able to get your dog to come down each step to meet you. Make sure you are petting and feeding treats. Keep the steps a fun thing for your dog. At first, help your dog a lot if she needs it, but then gradually offer less and less help so she learns how to navigate the steps on her own.

Some dogs will need a lot of work and practice with going one step at a time. Other dogs will follow you up and down rather quickly. Listen to your dog. She will tell you how comfortable she is and how much help she needs from you.

Teaching Fun Tricks!

Tricks are great fun to teach any dog! They let you show off how smart your dog is, but they are also great exercise for your dog physically and mentally. Here are some of our favorite tricks.

Beg

Dogs sitting on their haunches and begging are very cute. But the trick beg is also good for strengthening your dog's core body muscles. Wait until your dog is mature physically before teaching her to sit up and beg. Puppies usually aren't coordinated enough and their muscles are not fully formed.

Balance can be difficult for b/d dogs until they become familiar with the new sensations of their bodies being in a different position in space. Stay nearby and be ready to help steady your dog as she learns this trick.

Your dog will need to build up new muscles in order to stay in the beg position. Some dogs may sit up easily, but not be able to hold the position for very long in the beginning. Others will have a difficult time even getting into position. Take your time and take your cues from your dog as to how fast to proceed.

Begin with your dog in a sit position. You can use a lure to lead your dog's nose higher and higher up over her head. In order for her to balance properly, the lure will need to go up over her head and back towards her tail. At first, reward her for bringing her feet up off the floor even a little bit. If she seems to get the idea, slowly raise the lure and encourage her to come up off the floor a little bit more each time. Reward each attempt.

Sometimes it helps to sit the dog in a corner or with her back against your legs while you are standing to give her a solid support behind her. This can help her learn to balance in an upright position. As she gets better, you can position her a small distance from the wall so she has to rely more on her own muscles but the wall is still there to offer her a bit of support if she needs it.

Feed while she is up in the beg position if possible so she learns that this is the position that brings the rewards. Help her balance side to side and front to back, but don't expect any duration at this point. Remember that she needs to build up those new muscles.

You can also help your dog by lifting her front legs and holding them for her. Hold her front legs up so she is sitting in the beg position. Her back should be straight so she learns to balance on her own. Hold her there at first while you reward her. As she becomes more comfortable with staying in position, loosen your hold on her front legs slowly. She will learn to rely more on her own muscles to keep her balanced and less on your hand. Be sure her back is straight. If she is leaning forward into your hand, she will fall when you loosen your hold on her.

When your dog can get into the beg position by herself and balance there for a short time, you can begin to add a cue. Then wait for more duration to the position. Go slowly. If your dog is not successful, try again and ask for less time.

Paw and other paw

If your dog likes to paw at things, this is a great trick to start with. Start by making sure your dog is comfortable with you holding and handling her feet. If she doesn't like you touching her feet, she probably won't like this trick. So take some time with the handling games to teach her to enjoy having her feet touched if you need to.

I find this is easiest to teach from a sit position, so give your sit cue first. Place your hand behind your dog's front leg at the joint that is similar to our wrist. By tapping the back of this joint, you will probably notice that your dog begins to bend the joint and lift the leg slightly. At first, it may be just a very tiny shift in weight, but when you notice it, take the foot into your hand and feed several treats with the other hand. Try to feed while her paw is in your hand. Stop feeding when you release the paw.

You should find that as you practice, your dog will lift her paw much sooner when she feels the tapping. Try to pause just an extra second to see if your dog will raise her paw a bit higher before you take it. Your dog can't see to aim her own paw into your hand, so you will need to be ready to grab the foot as she lifts it.

The tapping can be diminished into two light taps on the back of your dog's leg. That can become the cue, or you can create a different cue if you'd like. Practice with both front legs, so your dog will pick up whichever leg you tap.

Many dogs enjoy playing with their paws and will lift up a paw to swipe at you when they are playing. If you are prepared with treats during times when your dog normally uses her paws, it can be very easy to teach this trick. Just take the paw into your hand while offering a treat. Soon, she will be offering her lifted paw to get another treat. Be careful, because your dog can't see what she's pawing at. Keep your face a safe distance away.

Some dogs will also paw at your hand if you hold a treat but don't let them have it right away. If your dog will paw at your hand to try to get the treat out, open your hand and let her have the treat as soon as she lifts her paw or touches your hand with her paw. Some dogs will also do this more readily from a down position, when their weight is not on the paw.

Once she is offering her paw easily, add a cue to the behavior. You don't want her pawing the air constantly hoping for a treat. Add the cue right before you anticipate your dog is going to lift her paw and always reward afterwards. When you start to use the cue, stop rewarding random paw lifting. Your dog will learn that only cued paw lifts get a treat, and the extra random pawing will start to extinguish.

Kiss

Some dogs like to give kisses and it will be easy for you to add a cue when they are in the mood. Add the cue immediately before she kisses you for the best result. You might be able to get her interested in kissing you and then give the cue in between kisses. Reward with lots of praise and petting. A treat might distract your dog from giving kisses, but you will know what works best for your dog.

If your dog does not usually give kisses, you can teach her to lick you on cue. You will need to find a sticky food that your dog will lick – peanut butter, honey, etc. Tuna water or canned cat food can be stinky too. Anything that will get your dog's attention will work. At first, put the food on the back of your hand and let your dog lick it off. When she will do this easily, offer your hand with less of the food on it, but still enough for your dog to be interested in. When she licks your hand, reward her with some of whatever food you are using.

When you think she understands that you want her to lick your hand, start to add the cue right before you present your hand to her. Then reward when she does the behavior. You can continue to decrease the food that is already on your hand by doing more than one repetition in a row. So, the first repetition will be with a bit of food on your hand, she will lick some of it off and you will reward. Then offer the same hand again without adding more food, etc.

You can teach your dog to lick your face if you want to. Dogs don't usually like having human faces right up in front of theirs, even b/d dogs. Dogs enjoy personal space and some of them will never learn to like being that close to a person's face. Also, always be careful since a dog kissing your face puts her teeth very close to your face. Beware of putting food on your face. Your b/d dog may decide to bite at the food instead of licking and she can't see to judge just how far away you are! That's why it's a good idea to teach this trick on your hand first!

Crawl

To teach your dog to crawl on her belly, begin with her in the down position. Use a food lure just in front of her nose. If you move the lure too quickly, your dog will stand up. Move it very slowly. Get your dog to stretch her neck out as far as she can and then see if you can get her to stretch just a little bit more. With any luck, she will shift her weight forward, which is the first movement of crawling. Reward her for that first little bit. As she gets more comfortable, lure her for a longer crawl.

When you can lure her to crawl several feet without her trying to stand up, add the cue. Give the crawl cue and then immediately lure her forward. When you start to fade out the lure, you will still need to provide your dog with direction of which way to crawl. My crawl cue is a gentle swipe forward off her paw and then a gentle patting on the floor ahead of her to keep her moving in the right direction.

Spin and twist

If you decide to teach your dog to spin in a circle, you should make sure to teach her to spin in both directions. Dogs usually prefer to spin in one direction over the other. By teaching her to spin in both directions, you will keep her flexible on both sides.

I use three quick taps on my dog's hip to signal a spin. Depending upon which hip I tap, I can signal a spin in each direction. I teach the cue from the beginning with this trick. Begin by lightly tapping your dog's hip on one side. She will most likely turn toward the touch to see what touched her. Be ready to feed a treat right away when she turns toward your hand.

When she is turning toward the tap easily, start to expect her to turn a little bit more toward your hand to get the treat. Soon she will be turning completely in a circle to get her reward. If you are having trouble getting your dog to turn around, try the spin in the other direction and see if it's easier for your dog to turn that way.

When you want your dog to spin in the direction that is harder for her, be patient and reward more often for small turns at first. As her muscles on that side become more flexible, she will be able to turn more and more. The tap on one hip that originally caused her to turn and investigate can now become the signal for the trick.

You can also teach this trick by luring your dog to turn in a circle with a treat. Once she is turning easily for the treat, you can add the cue.

Roll over both ways

Rolling over will come more easily to some dogs than others. Some dogs enjoy rolling and playing on their backs and others feel threatened by it. Work slowly until you know how your dog will react. The easiest way to teach this is to get your dog relaxed by giving a belly rub. As she relaxes, you can gradually roll her more and more onto her side and then onto her back while still rubbing the belly. Don't rush the roll at first. Just focus on keeping your dog relaxed and enjoying the experience of the belly rub and being on her back. As you stop rubbing the belly and release your dog, try to release her so she continues the roll over onto her other side and then reward. Don't worry about adding a cue until this process is going smoothly and your dog is relaxed.

Another technique which you can try is to lead your dog over with a treat. With your dog in a down position, you will probably notice that her weight is over on one hip and her rear legs are sticking out to one side of her body. Begin with the treat on the side where her legs are sticking out. Put the treat very close to her elbow on that side so she has to tuck her head close to her neck to get the treat. As she tucks her head close, her shoulders should begin to roll towards the floor on the opposite side until she is lying on one side. Very slowly move the treat to lead her nose back over her shoulders so she rolls even more onto her back. Then you will need to lead her nose with the treat so it is going toward the floor behind her. If you can slowly lead her nose over her shoulders and back toward the floor, the rest of her body should follow.

When you have the roll over going smoothly in both directions, you can begin to add your cues. Present your cue and then immediately begin to help your dog roll over. You can use the same cue but on different sides of the dog to signal a roll in either direction. With repetition, you will be able to give the cue and help with the roll less and less until she starts to respond on her own when you give the cue.

Roll out a mat

A cute trick is to have your dog roll out a carpet mat with her nose. Choose a mat that is able to be rolled up and will stay in that shape. Roll the mat up and feed your dog treats from next to the roll on the floor. Put the treats down on the floor for her to find, not from your hand. Place the treats down closer and closer to the rolled up mat. As your dog eats the treats, her nose will begin to push against the mat.

The next step is to place some treats just inside the rolled up part of the mat. As your dog smells for the treat, help her to unroll the mat and get the treats inside. Help her less each time until she is pushing the roll on her own. By placing more treats inside the mat as you roll it up, you can teach your dog to unroll the entire mat while she hunts for treats.

As she gets the idea and is unrolling the mat all the way to the end, start to space out the placement of treats so she has to push open more of the mat before finding the treats. Let her find a treat early on in the pushing, then about half way, and put a lot of treats at the end. Eventually, you can roll up the mat and only put treats at the end of the roll.

Into/onto a box

Using a lure, you can teach your dog to climb into or onto a low box. Make sure the box you choose is sturdy and won't tip or collapse under your dog's weight. Luring will help her learn to get into or onto the box. Reward for her putting one foot inside, then two, three and finally all four. Then fade the lure until you are using your empty hand to lead her into or onto the box. You can do this by gently touching her in the direction you want her to follow you.

Once she is doing the behavior the way you want, add a cue. Practice it for a while with the cue first, then luring the behavior with your open hand. You may always need to use your hand to help your dog line up to get on the box safely because she won't be able to see it. Once she's lined up, you can give the cue to get into or onto the box.

Some Other Activities Your B/D Dog May Enjoy

There are a multitude of dog activities out there. With a little creativity, your blind and deaf dog should be able to participate in many of them. Here are a few of them that we enjoy.

Therapy, READ programs

Dogs doing therapy or READ program work go with their handlers to libraries, schools, hospitals, nursing homes, and other similar venues, to visit with and bring comfort to others. It is very demanding work emotionally for the dogs, and not every dog is suitable. Your dog must be very comfortable in new environments, with new people and dogs, and being restrained and touched all over her body. It's important for a therapy dog to enjoy her work and be relaxed doing it.

If you feel your dog is suitable to work as a therapy dog, it is best to find an organized therapy dog group to work with. There are local groups and national groups. Most groups require the dog and handler to have some training and go through an evaluation of some sort. Most groups then offer some type of liability coverage to their registered teams in exchange for a small yearly fee.

You will need to check with each organization to see if they will evaluate your b/d dog. I have found from experience that sometimes a local therapy dog organization is more accepting of including a b/d dog, but you will need to speak to different groups until you find a good fit for you and your dog.

K9 Nosework

It's easy to get started with the sport of k9 nosework. There are classes popping up everywhere. Nosework is a fun activity whether you decide to do it just for fun, or you decide to progress to competition levels.

Dogs learn to search for specific odors in progressively challenging situations. There are indoor, outdoor, vehicle and container searches.

K9 nosework is becoming very popular. It is a sport that any dog can do and it is a great enrichment activity to have fun with your dog.

Trick dog titles

Do More With Your Dog offers trick dog titles of various levels. They provide you with an extensive list of tricks for each level. You can choose which of those tricks you feel your dog is able to do. Once you teach your dog the specified number of tricks from each level, you can apply for a title! Super fun!

Tracking

Tracking may be an activity that you and your b/d dog can enjoy, as long as you ensure the dog's safety in an outdoor environment. The sport relies on your dog's ability to follow a human scent trail with her nose.

CGC

The American Kennel Club offers a Canine Good Citizen test and certificate to any dog and handler. There are a series of ten activities that make up the CGC. It is meant to show that your dog is friendly and accepting towards people and dogs, can be handled, and knows basic obedience and manners skills.

Treasure CGC

Resources
From the Author

My website with some helpful training articles about blind/deaf dogs:

www.your-inner-dog.com

My blog about living with and training blind/deaf dogs:

www.your-inner-dog.blogspot.com

My beautiful models for this book –
Vegas, Treasure, Jasmine, and Grace.

Other B/D Resources You May Find Helpful

Blind/deaf dog information

The blind and deaf dog's guidebook website

> www.pawstoadopt.com/blindanddeafdogs

Lethal Whites UK

> http://lethalwhitesuk.webs.com

Info pages on deaf, blind, and blind-deaf dogs

> http://deafdogsforever.weebly.com

Blind-deaf-dogs yahoo list

> http://groups.yahoo.com/group/blind-deaf-dogs

Lethal whites yahoo list

> http://groups.yahoo.com/group/LethalWhiteAussieRescue

Here are some links to pages showing **various eye defects** that can occur in double merle dogs:

> http://www.ashgi.org/color/eyedefects.htm

Training with **vibration collars**

> http://www.deafdogs.org/training/vibratrain.php

Where to find tools and equipment

How to make a halo collar for a blind dog

> www.ehow.com/how_4841270_collar-blind-dog.html

> http://www.handicappedpets.com/pet-care-articles/handicapped-pet-equipment/163-blind-dog-hoop-harness.html

http://www.blinddogs.net/blind_dog_collar_plan.html

Halo necklace

http://www.halosforpaws.com

Apparel for blind and deaf dogs

http://thankfulpaws.com/index.htm

Angel vest

http://angelvest.homestead.com

Doggles

http://doggles.com

Hats for dogs

www.fouronthefloorpetwear.com/partycollars.html

Quick release martingale collars

http://www.dogsupplies.com/products/Red-Adjustable-Chain-Quick-Release-Martingale-Dog-Collar.html

Thundershirt

http://www.thundershirt.com

Puppy bumpers

http://www.puppybumpers.net

DAP products: spray, collar, plug ins

http://www.petcomfortzone.com

http://www.amazon.com/Adaptil-Appeasing-Pheromone-Collar-Medium/dp/B000HPVH78

Rescue remedy

http://www.bachflower.com/rescue-remedy-pets-bach-flower

http://www.bachrescueremedypet.com

T shirts

http://www.cafepress.com/+deaf-and-blind-dog+gifts

Tag covers for white dogs

> http://www.pawspetboutique.com/pet-tag-silencers

> http://www.thefind.com/pets/info-pet-tag-silencer

Manners Minder

> http://www.premierpet.com/View.aspx?page=dogs/products/behavior/mannersminder/productdescription

Links to helpful techniques and workshops

Healing Touch for Animals®

> http://www.healingtouchforanimals.com/Default.asp

TTouch®

> http://www.ttouch.com

Dog body language

> http://www.aspca.org/pet-care/virtual-pet-behaviorist/dog-behavior/canine-body-language

> http://www.petprofessionalguild.com/DogBodylanguage

> http://info.drsophiayin.com/free-poster-on-body-language-in-dogs

> http://www.diamondsintheruff.com/diagrams.html

> http://avsabonline.org/blog/view/ladder-of-aggression

Child and dog safety for parents

> http://www.doggonesafe.com/dog_bite_prevention

> http://familypaws.com

> http://www.livingwithkidsanddogs.com/resources.html

Dog park safety and info

http://www.apdt.com/petowners/park/etiquette.aspx

https://www.apdt.com/petowners/park/body-language

Choosing the right dog for you

http://www.apdt.com/petowners/gettingadog

Dog-proofing your home

http://www.petco.com/Content/ArticleList/Article/32/1/363/Dog-Proofing-Checklist.aspx

http://www.paws.org/puppy-proofing.html

Blind dogs

http://www.blinddogs.com

http://www.blinddogs.net

http://www.blinddogrescue.com

http://www.blinddogsupport.com

http://www.blinddogrescue.com

http://blinddeafdogs.blogspot.com

Deaf dogs

http://www.deafdogs.org

http://deafdogsrock.com

http://www.ourdeafdogs.com

http://www.deafdogsneedavoice.com

http://blinddeafdogs.blogspot.com

Appendix One –
Touch Cues

Here are some ideas for touch cues (but of course you can use your own signals) to get you started:

Good girl: petting

Clicker/marker signal: quick double tap to withers, top of shoulder area at base of neck

Stop that: one finger brought down gently but firmly on top of bridge of nose twice

OK, release cue: three quick open hand pats on her side

Pay attention: a light touch anywhere on her body will bring her around to pay attention and see what I want

All done, no more: using one hand open wide, palm against her cheek, I move that hand back and forth so she can feel it on her face.

Do your business, potty cue: three taps on the top of her tail done once already outside in the toileting area.

Sit: tap or light pressure on rump at top of tail

Down: three light taps on front toes of one foot or other

Down stay: gentle but firm pressure on shoulders (done with open palm) toward ground after she is already down, done three times

Sit stay: one hand on top of shoulders after she is already sitting, second hand gives gentle but firm pressure on chest three times

Let's go this way: brush fingers (palm up) under chin outward toward direction I want her to come with me

Come: a gentle blowing on her and she will follow my breath to come to me. Also use a vibration cue of stomping on floor or wooden deck.

Stand: light touch with my open hand near her stifle (knee) and she will stand up from a sit position or remain standing while I groom her

Stand stay: gentle but firm pressure on her shoulders with my open palm toward the ground once she is standing, done three times.

Leash cues: given when walking, can use solid leash or flexible leash. Gentle pressure in direction you want to go signals turns, can signal speeds, starts and halts.

Put front feet up on me or object: brush my open hand upward from her chest to her chin toward the object. Done when she is facing and very close to the object so she can find it with her feet.

Spin or turn right and left: three taps on the hip on the side I want her to turn towards. I use three taps for a complete spin in a circle, and one tap for just a turn toward that direction.

Find it: for searching nosework, I kneel behind Treasure and use both hands to cradle her face facing her forward. I bounce my hands while holding her face and then release her to go search.

Shake hands: tap the back of the leg I want her to raise (near the back of her wrist), once she raises it, then take it in my hand and shake it

Eat, mealtime: with my fingers, I tap lightly three times on the front of her chin, near her teeth.

Car: I use a closed fist beginning at one of her shoulders, moving upward over her withers and ending at the other shoulder, remaining in contact with her for the entire movement.

Come inside from yard: if at night time, I blink the porch light off, pause and then on again. By the time I open the door, she is there waiting to come in.

Let's play: flat hand on back of head and ruffled up her neck and over the top of her nose

Off: flat palm placed on top of her head and firm but gentle pressure downward toward floor, not hitting the dog.

Wait: touch forehead with index finger, pause for a moment

CPSIA information can be obtained
at www.ICGtesting.com
Printed in the USA
FSHW012013160619
59112FS

9 781495 391552